ROGER BREWER

Should a Christian Wear Purple Sweat Socks?

Should a Christian wear purple sweat socks?

James Watkins

Wesley Press
Indianapolis, Indiana

Published by Wesley Press, 1987
Printed in the United States of America.
International Standard Book Number: 0-89827-039-1

Dedicated to my wife, Lois (who has helped me accept people of different-colored socks)

Contents

Foreword
Keith Drury

How do you know if something's right or wrong? You could simply listen to your parents. How about the rules of the Church? Maybe you could take an informal poll of all your friends. These methods may be the most common way to determine whether something is right or wrong.

A much better way is to use God's Word. However, that's not as easy as it appears at first sight. Not long ago, I saw a bumper sticker announcing "God said it, it's true, that settles it for me." The trouble is, the Bible is not completely clear on a lot of things. Sure, it forbids premarital sex, drunkenness, hate, bitterness, stealing, and lying. But there are a lot of "gray areas" in today's world. What does the Bible say about R-rated movies? How about dancing? If a person is a Christian and he sneaks out in the woods and smokes a cigarette, will he quit being a Christian? Is listening to rock music a sin?

These are the kind of things this book deals with. Not that it gives you a handy list of permanent do's and don'ts. It has a far more thoughtful approach than that. Reading this book will give you principles right from the Bible to help you make a decision. Some of these questionable or controversial practices divide us. This book will help us all see the matter of "questionable things" from the Bible's perspective.

I loved the book! I think you will too!

Keith Drury
General Secretary of Youth
The Wesleyan Church

I. Who says purple sweat socks are right or wrong?

"Should a Christian wear purple sweat socks then?" Mike was always asking ridiculous questions during youth meetings, so I gave him a let's-get-serious look.

"I'm serious, Pastor Jim. We're trying to figure out what the Bible means when it says 'dress modestly.' And you said, 'Modest clothing doesn't draw undue attention to itself.' Take a look at Jennifer's! I bet she has to recharge those things every night! So, should she wear bright purple sweat socks?"

Fortunately we were out of time, so I could use the famous delaying tactic, "That brings up some excellent questions. Let's talk about it next week."

After order had been restored and a quick closing prayer, Kimberly asked to see me after the meeting. She fought back the tears as she sat in my office.

"I've got to know if —— is right or wrong! I'm just so confused that I don't know what I believe anymore. Sure, I know what my church believes and what my parents think. I just don't know what I believe anymore.''

The young woman took a deep breath and strained to regain control.

''I guess I just want to know what you think.''

''I can't tell you.''

''Come on, Pastor Jim. Isn't that what you went to school for?''

''Look. I have some very strong opinions on ——. And it's very tempting to tell you those views. But you would just have *another* person's values. What you need to do is see what *God* has to say about it. And if you don't find any specific references to ——, here's a list of seven principles St. Paul gives for determining if something is right or wrong when Scripture is silent on the topic. You and God work through each checkpoint, and then you'll not only know what you believe, but *why* you believe it.''

Since then, I've handed out several hundred mimeographed copies of ''Biblical Principles For Thinking For Yourself.'' As I talk to teens in churches and camps I become more convinced that what we don't need is another sermon or book on the hot issue of the day. We need a tool for each of us to decide ''Is —— right for *me?*'' And once I've made a decision, how do I act toward those who believe just the opposite?

You won't find the answer to the burning question, ''Should a Christian wear purple sweat socks?'' But this book will help you sort out the values and beliefs that shape your life. It's designed as a workbook for you and God to talk through the issues and decisions you're struggling with. So every time you see the phrase ''purple sweat socks'' just substitute the specific issue you're struggling with, and then you will discover if it is right or wrong for *you.*

Because if you don't think for yourself, somebody else will!

Manufacturers and the media

The president of ''Sock It To You Industries'' just

found out the company has three million surplus purple sweat socks in the warehouse. He knows he has to sell a lot of socks to keep in business.

The president of the TV network also knows he has to sell a lot of advertising to stay in business. The two get together over a one-hundred-dollar lunch and "purple sweat socks" become a national fad. The manufacturer and advertiser care nothing about the aesthetic appeal of purple sweat socks. They may not even care if they're good for you. They do care that both of their businesses make a profit.

The president of the network has another consideration. His Neilson ratings must be high enough so advertisers will buy time. No ratings = no advertisers = no network. The network cares little about the morality of its programming – only that enough people will watch it. If purple sweat socks will boost ratings, you'll see purple sweat socks in every sitcom and TV drama. If they don't, you'll never see another one on network TV.

The same is true with record producers, book publishers, movie makers, newspapers, and even some television evangelists. They will push whatever values, beliefs, and morals they think will sell.

The government

Let's say purple sweat socks have become a national obsession. Unemployment has dropped below 1% as abandoned automobile plants are now producing millions of socks each year. These are great economic times. But suddenly the surgeon general reveals that purple sweat socks may cause cancer in laboratory animals.

The discussion (and lobbying by the purple sweat sock manufacturers) on Capitol Hill doesn't focus on the health and well-being of the wearers. Unfortunately in government also, morality is often spelled m-o-n-e-y. Just recently a bill to require seat belts on school buses was rejected. The reason – the idea was not "cost-effective." Plus, most congressmen will be thinking of their reelection campaign when they vote on the issue.

And because the TV news also depends on advertising bucks, chances are you won't hear much about the research results either. They don't want "Sock It To You Industries" to pull out their billion-dollar advertising contract.

Remember, just because it's in print or in the 6:00 news doesn't mean it's necessarily true.

Public school

If you've had biology or psychology, you've already discovered that God's principles have little place in the classroom. Even admitting you believe in God often gets strange looks from teachers and friends. We'll talk more about the influence of school and what you can do about it.

Parents and friends

Unlike manufacturers and the media, parents and friends have nothing to gain financially from you. In fact keeping you fed, watered, and clothed is an economic drain on Mom and Dad. They had you, not just for a tax deduction, but because they wanted someone to love. So you can be sure that their motives for wanting you to brush your teeth, be in by midnight, and date the right people are pure.

Pure, but not perfect. They have no previous experience in raising children – only on-the-job training. And few have doctor's degrees in theology, philosophy, ethics, and logic to perfectly answer, to your satisfaction, the now-famous question "Should a Christian wear purple sweat socks?"

No, they don't have all the answers, but they have your best interest at heart. We'll talk about living with non-Christian parents later.

The church

Heather was one of the sharpest girls in our youth

group. And yet the idea of "thinking for herself" was frightening.

"Look, Pastor. I come here for answers and all you give me are these questions!"

Heather is now with a controversial church group. (Several have died in this church because its leader refuses to allow "his children" to receive medical attention.) She looks to this powerful leader for her day-to-day decision-making. Heather and the entire congregation are no longer thinking for themselves. Instead, all the "answers" are now neatly provided for her.

Now obviously, this is a rare and extreme case. The church *is* the best place to find God's answers to our questions. But even in church we need to be cautious. Well-meaning pastors and teachers have attempted to help new Christians mature by providing them with the church's answers to the various issues. And in most cases, the answers were scripturally based.

But rather than becoming sensitive to God's Spirit and knowing Him better, the young Christians have only become spiritually dependent on the church. I'm convinced that those who have been "spoon-fed" their beliefs will eventually abandon those beliefs when the pressure to conform is heavy, if they have not personally thought through each value and belief.

God

I'm *not* urging you to burn your TV, boycott your school, picket Washington or leave your church. I just want you to be aware that many people and organizations are attempting to answer questions for you. But God makes us personally responsible for our decisions, our values and beliefs.

While friends and parents can love us unconditionally, with no thought of financial return, they don't have all the answers. God not only loves us just the way we are, He offers us His wisdom. Read Romans

11:33–12:2 before continuing. (Come on, don't just sit there, get up and get your Bible. If you open your New Testament in the middle, you'll be at Romans – or close by. As we work through this book, keep your Bible handy.)

God does want to help you make decisions on the issues you're facing.

Who says purple sweat socks are right or wrong for *you?* Is it advertisers? Is it your Sunday school teacher? Is it your best friend? Is it Mom and Dad? Is it God?

What do YOU really believe about purple sweat socks? Sorting it all out is hard (and sometimes frightening) work.

I was in high school when I laced up my first pair of rink roller skates. The thick matting helped keep me somewhat upright, but then came the slippery wooden floor. Totally embarrassed, I hung on to the rail and slowly slipped along. I was starting to regain a bit of confidence (and equilibrium), when suddenly I found myself going 30 MPH in the middle of the rink.

"Isn't this much better than hanging on to that rail!"

It was Phil the youth sponsor pushing me along as we wove through slower traffic.

"Take me back to the rail!"

"You're never going to have any fun depending on that rail. And besides you'll look dumb trying to skate with Patti – one arm around her and another around it. You're doing pretty well, so I'm going to let go of you on the next straightaway."

"But I can't turn. I'll be flattened against the wall. Phil? Phil! Phil!!!"

"Dear Lord, I'm too young to die. Are you listening? Help!"

Suddenly (just as I began to see my life pass before me) I felt my feet turning and my body leaning into the curve.

"Praise the Lord, we did it!" The night wasn't totally miraculous — I did have my share of spills! But by night's end, I was thoroughly enjoying this new freedom.

Attempting to work out your own beliefs and values without totally depending on the church, Mom and Dad, or friends is equally frightening, and yet equally satisfying. And you'll probably discover that Mom and Dad and the church were right all along.

But the important thing will be these are now *your* beliefs. Not something you've been spoon-fed. And when the pressure to conform is on, you'll be able to defend your beliefs with something far more substantial than "Well . . . ah . . . my church believes . . . ah . . ."

Dr. Francis Schaeffer shares his struggle at this point in *True Spirituality.*

"I faced a spiritual crisis in my own life. I had become a Christian from agnosticism many years before. After that I had become pastor for ten years. Gradually, however, a problem came to me — the problem of reality. My own reality was less than it had been in the early days after I had become a Christian. I realized in honesty I had to go back [to agnosticism] and rethink my whole position.

"I walked, prayed, and thought through what the Scriptures taught as well as reviewing my own reasons for being a Christian. I saw again that there were totally sufficient reasons to know that the infinite-personal God does exist and that Christianity is true."

I pray that as you walk, pray, and think through what the Scriptures teach concerning the issue you're struggling with, that God will give you His wisdom.

See to it that no one takes you captive through hollow and deceptive philosophy, which depends on human tradition and the basic principles of this world rather than on Christ (Colossians 2:8).

For further reading . . .

> 2 Peter 2:1-3
> 1 John 2:18-27

How to be Your Own Selfish Pig (and other ways you've been brainwashed) by Susan Schaeffer

Lord, What's Really Important? by Fritz Ridenour (Regal Books)

Making the Most of Your Mind by Stephen B. Douglas and Lee Roddy (Here's Life Publishers).

Escape From Reason by Francis Schaeffer (Inter-Varsity Press)

II. What does God's Word say about purple sweat socks?

1. Specific principles

*I*f any of you lacks wisdom, he should ask God, who gives generously to all without finding fault, and it will be given to him (James 1:5).

"OK, where can you find out if purple sweat socks are right or wrong?" Jennifer asked the following week. (I noticed she was wearing hot pink socks to this youth meeting.)

"The first place I'd look would be the Bible. It's not a dusty piece of literature filled with myths. It's reliable and relevant now for today's issues."

"But aren't there a lot of 'holy books' that claim they have the answers too?"

"Right, Mike. But all the others rely on visions and dreams written down by the cult's leader. Josh McDowell has spent years documenting the accuracy of Scripture with historical and archeological evidence. He points out that, 'Christianity appeals to facts of history . . . the most patent and accessible of data. Christ is a fact of history as real as any other.' "

Mike's hand was up again. "But can't you prove just about anything with the Bible?"

"Right! Even biblical truth can be dangerous when not handled properly. I remember my first jackknife. It was bright yellow (probably so I wouldn't lose it) and was the sharpest object I had ever been allowed to touch.

"I watched in awe as my dad showed me the proper way to open it, how to always cut away from myself, and how to sharpen it to a razor edge. With great fear and respect I whittled my first stick, carefully following my dad's warnings and instructions . . .

". . . until I started becoming familiar with it. I discovered I could shave the peach fuzz off the back of my arm with it. I discovered I could hold it by the blade and flick it into a board – just like on the late-night spy movies. And I discovered it could send you to the hospital for stitches!

"Hebrews 4:12 warns that *the word of God is living and active. Sharper than any double-edged sword, it penetrates even to dividing soul and spirit, joints and marrow* . . . We can get hurt, and hurt others by not correctly handling *the word of truth* (2 Timothy 2:15).

"For the first few years of my Christian life, I used the 'Columbus Bible Study Method' – discover and land on a verse. I would close my eyes, pray 'God, I need an answer about ——,' open my Bible, plop my finger down, and claim the 'landed on' verse as my answer." Several heads nodded they used the same method.

"There is the old joke about the man who also used the 'Columbus Bible Study Method.' 'Lord, I really want to know what you want me to do.' He closes his eyes, opens his Bible and plops his finger on Matthew 27:5 – *Judas . . . went away and hanged himself.*"

Several groaned. "I said it was old. But it gets worse. 'Lord, this can't be right!' He tries again, this time landing on Luke 10:37. *Go and do likewise.*

" 'I'll try it just one more time.' He opens his Bible

the third time, stabs his finger down, peers out one eye to read John 13:27, *What you . . . do, do quickly!"*

More groans. "Here's the point. God has given us the Bible, not so we can know *it*, but that we can know *Him*. We may know the names of the twelve disciples, the books of the Bible, and fifty memory verses, but know very little about God's ideas, values, and beliefs.

"As we dig through His Word, keep in mind it is not merely to see God's views on current issues, but to see God, to see ourselves and allow Him to change us into His likeness.

"Here's what 2 Timothy 3:16-17 says about it. *All Scripture is God-breathed and is useful for teaching, rebuking, correcting and training in righteousness, so that the man of God may be thoroughly equipped for every good work."*

The rest of the evening was spent discussing ways to understand God's Word more clearly. If you're having trouble discovering God's truth in the Bible, try some of these tips.

1. Pick a time for maximum alertness.

For years I lived under tremendous guilt that I was not up at 5:00 having devotions. At every youth meeting, church service and camp meeting I got the impression that the only time God had open on His appointment calendar was before 7:00.

I finally discovered that God has created two kinds of people – morning people and night people. (I've also discovered that morning people usually marry night people!) While I'm at the office at 8:00, I am rarely fully conscious of what is going on until around 9:00.

So my best effective time to spend with God is after the late news – the kids are in bed, the phone isn't ringing, and besides I have the whole night for scripture to soak into my subconscious. Whatever you discover is the best time for you, is the best time to meet with God. (He works a twenty-four hour shift!)

2. Get away from distractions.

I wrote this book in the shower. (Unfortunately a waterproof word processor hasn't been invented, so I had to do the typing in the office.) But in the shower I'm relaxed, free from the oxygen restrictions of a coat and tie, and no one is saying, "Can you look over this manuscript?" It's just me, and God, and the Water-Pik massager.

I also do most of my Bible reading in the bathroom. Everyone needs a special place to get alone with God and His Word. Christ spent forty days in the wilderness before He began His ministry. Paul spent three years in Arabia. God can use our "wildernesses" of illness or just boredom to share His insights with us. Fifteen minutes of undistracted time with God is worth more than an hour trying to read on the school bus or during study hall.

3. Pray.

Ask God to give you special sensitivity to His Word. Ask Him to show you what *He* wants you to discover. Pray for wisdom. Read the verse again at the beginning of this chapter. He will give us special wisdom if we'll just ask.

4. Study His Word.

The Bible was originally written in Hebrew, Aramaic, and Greek. Since few of us are fluent in any of these ancient languages, God has blessed us with many fine translations and paraphrases.

The *King James* (or Authorized) *Version* has been a long-time favorite. However, it was translated in 1611 and has been revised many times to remove no-longer-used words. (No copy in print today is exactly like the original of 400 years ago.)

Some have objected that "modern translations don't sound like God. They sound like the man on the street." The New Testament was written for the "man on the street." Koine Greek was the working class language of fishermen, tax collectors and men "in the street."

Today's translations have the advantage of recent archeological finds (such as the Dead Sea Scrolls) that shed new light on the original meanings.

Plus, modern translations are also arranged by paragraphs. Chapter and verse divisions were not inspired of God. Chapter divisions were created in A.D. 1250 by the church, and the verse divisions were made in 1551 by a printer. (The man was obviously not a theologian, or even an editor, since he thoughtlessly broke up thoughts and concepts.)

The *New American Standard Bible* is a word-for-word translation out of the original languages and maintains the literary flavor of the *KJV.*

The *New International Version* is also a word-for-word translation, but reads more smoothly than the NASB. It is rapidly becoming a favorite translation throughout evangelical churches.

Several good paraphrase editions are also available. *The Living Bible* is by far the most popular and is excellent for seeing the overall theme of a book or chapter, but was not intended for study of specific verses or words.

Kenneth Taylor, who paraphrased the Bible, cautions, "Copies of this book should be in every Christian household as a companion to favored translations in use in that home. Every member of the family needs this paraphrase to use alongside of . . . standard translations. For study purposes, a paraphrase should be checked against a rigid translation."

The best way to study Scripture, and in turn discover God's thoughts on particular issues, would be to master Hebrew, Aramaic, and Greek and read from the ancient manuscripts. Since that could be a full-time job, we can do the next best thing by using the most current and accurate translations of God's Word.

You're probably familiar with "Little House on the Prairie" reruns. We'll use their "homesteading" approach in searching for answers to today's issues and decisions.

(1) Survey the land

We need to be constant readers of the Word – not just looking for specific verses for a specific issue. One college professor suggested we burn all our concordances.

"If you have to look through the entire Bible each time you want to prove something, you'll see what *God* has to say, and not just some verse to prove what *you* want to say."

He's right – with over 23,000 verses to choose from, you can find a verse to prove your point on any current controversy. That's why getting the "big picture" gives us the verse in its context.

Sometimes we need to go as far as the context of the entire book – or the whole of Scripture to find the true meaning. To prove this point, I asked my youth group to read the book of Ecclesiastes and develop their own cult using specific verses. The results were incredible!

One "cult's" members were required to visit the Humane Society on a weekly basis to hold services for the strays since, "The fate of the sons of man and the fate of beasts is the same. Indeed they all have the same breath and there is not advantage for man over beast, for all is vanity" (Ecclesiastes 3:19). The cult's leader was also to be a German Shepherd!

These teens realized the importance of reading large portions of Scripture at one time. In doing so, they realized that Ecclesiastes is the journal of a man's spiritual wanderings.

We can't limit our investigation to a verse, a chapter, or even a book of Scripture. We need to see themes, emphases, and correlations. In preparing this book, I read the New Testament through several times. And each time God seemed to bring new concepts into focus.

As you're reading, ask God to direct your attention to those narratives or teachings that would apply to the issue you're struggling with. You may want to pencil in the margin the name of the issue you're considering, but KEEP MOVING!

When you are stumped by a verse, simply put a question mark in the margin and keep reading. The context of the passage may answer it. Remember you're trying to get the "big picture" at this stage – don't be jumping up and down to get your Bible dictionary or call the pastor.

And there are a lot of stars in the margins of my Bible. They mean "Ouch! I needed that." But even they don't detour me in my search for the

theme,
context,
key words,
connecting words,
the cultural setting,
mood,
and person addressed

in the book or books. The problem with grabbing the concordance and trying to look up the issue is

1– The issue is probably not specifically listed in your concordance.

2– If you do find it, you probably won't see the context that holds the seemingly differing arguments together.

(2) Stake it out

Only after getting an overview of the entire landscape are we ready to unpack the excavation tools.

Cross-reference Bibles are invaluable for tracing the associated scriptures of a related topic. "Chain" Bibles are very popular with hundreds of topics in logical sequence so you can follow each through your Bible.

Bible dictionaries are more like mini-encyclopedias with articles on people, places, themes, events, culture and history. I find myself using my Bible dictionary more than any of my other study books.

Concordances. While I wholeheartedly agree with the college prof, there *are* sixty-six books, 1,189 chapters, and 23,214 verses. I haven't burned my concordance yet!

Commentaries. Save these as a "last resort." They take all the fun out of "thinking for yourself." It is not until I feel I've exhausted my insights into a portion of Scripture that I open one up. (And they often avoid handling the really tough issues anyway.)

I'd suggest getting a one-volume commentary that is very close to your own church's doctrine and theology, and a second one that is totally opposite. It will give you a broader view of God and His plan and force you to clarify your own beliefs on various doctrines.

(3) Settle in

Mark Twain quipped, "It is not the parts of the Bible I don't understand that bother me, it is the parts I do understand." The real problem is not in trying to find out God's view on a particular subject – the problem is putting those discoveries into practice.

For the time will come when men will not put up with sound doctrine. Instead, to suit their own desires, they will gather around them a great number of teachers to say what their itching ears want to hear. They will turn their ears away from the truth and turn aside to myths (2 Timothy 4:3-4).

As we read we must be constantly asking,

1. How does this apply to the issues or decision at hand?

2. How does it apply to *me?*

Some final cautions in *rightly handling the word.* There are some scriptures that definitely do *not* apply to us. Paul was very careful to separate his personal beliefs from God's eternal truth. Throughout his letters he clarifies his statements, *I say this (I, not the Lord)* and *I have no command from the Lord, but I give a judgment as one who by the Lord's mercy is trustworthy* (1 Corinthians 7:12a, 25).

There is also controversy about the authenticity of John 7:53–8:11 and Mark 16:9-20. These portions are not in the most reliable early manuscripts. The Mark portion implies that *every* believer will be driving out demons, speaking in new tongues, handling snakes and drinking poison with no harm, and healing every disease.

And be careful about drawing beliefs from biblical history. You'll be reading this in Cell Block 5 if you use Judges 19 as an example of how to deal with crime in the streets. And while David was "a man after God's own heart," his political strategies will win you a term in the "Big House" rather than the White House. These are extreme examples. But I have heard too many sermons promoting personal beliefs that use a biblical story to prove their point.

Finally, the Jews claimed each scripture had four separate meanings.

1. Literal, factual meaning
2. Suggested meaning
3. Meaning arrived at after long and careful investigation
4. Allegorical or mystical meaning.

Number four was the Pharisees' favorite. But each step away from number one allows for more and more human influence, error, and heresy. God's Word most often says exactly what it means!

Paul was aware of this problem when he wrote in 1 Corinthians 4:6 *Do not go beyond what is written.* I wish each church had a banner like the one I saw in southern Indiana.

Where the Bible speaks, we speak.
Where the Bible is silent, we are silent.
Amen.

For further reading . . .

Adam Clarke's Commentary on the Holy Bible – one volume (Baker)

The Daily Study Bible by William Barclay (Westminster)

The Matthew Henry Commentary – one volume (Zondervan)

Independent Bible Study by Irving L. Jensen

The New Testament and Wycliffe Bible Commentary – one volume (Moody Press)

Prayer: Conversing with God by Rosalind Rinker (Zondervan)

The Zondervan Pictorial Bible Dictionary edited by Merrill C. Tenney (Zondervan)

2. General principles

(1) Is it beneficial and constructive?

(2) Is it not mastering me?

P astor Jim, I looked in my dad's concordance and I can't even find 'sock' in the Bible. I did find a lot about 'purple' though. It must be one of His favorite colors since most of the stuff in the temple was purple."

"Good work, Mike! Many of the issues you're struggling with won't be listed in a concordance – they have come out of recent scientific research. But I'm convinced that God was aware of every 'new' issue that would come up, and has provided some broad principles for many of them.

"Let's turn to 1 Corinthians 10 and Matthew 15."

"Everything is permissible" – but not everything is beneficial. *"Everything is permissible"* – but not everything is constructive. . . . *"Everything is permissible for me"* – but I will not be mastered by anything (1 Corinthians 10:23, 6:12b).

What goes into a man's mouth does not make

him "unclean," but what comes out of his mouth, that is what makes him "unclean." . . . Don't you see that whatever enters the mouth goes into the stomach and then out of the body? But the things that come out of the mouth come from the heart, and these make a man "unclean" (Matthew 15:11, 17-18).

Christ and Paul declare that no "thing" is good or evil, right or wrong, moral or immoral, clean or unclean. Moral values come from the heart of man.

Purple sweat socks come from cute little lambs chasing cute little butterflies through sunny green meadows. That sounds harmless enough. Clippings from their spring haircut is processed into yarn, dyed, and knitted together by "Sock It To You Industries" to keep your feet warm while walking to school in the winter. And that sounds harmless enough.

But there will always be the Steve Browns. One day, during sixth-grade recess, Steve discovered he could fill his socks with rocks (after he had taken them off) and terrorize the playground with "sock rockets." They were a short-lived fad, however, after Steve slung one through the Kindergarten window. That wasn't so harmless.

Now, should Westlake School sue "Sock It To You Industries" for damages? Of course not! Purple sweat socks are morally neutral. It is the *user* who is morally responsible for how they are used.

It is the same with new scientific discoveries and medical procedures. On one hand they may promise new hope for our world, and on the other hand, hold the potential for destroying our world.

Paul emphasizes this point as he looks at several hot issues of his day. He gives seven ways to judge if a current issue is good or evil, right or wrong, moral or immoral, clean or unclean for each individual.

If the Bible is COMPLETELY SILENT on the particular issue, I must look within myself to decide if something is right or wrong. But that's frustrating to some! They would rather have a direct answer to "Is

—— right or wrong?'' than a seven-point checklist. But all of us have different backgrounds, temperaments, personalities, social and cultural standards, strengths and weaknesses.

Some "thing" may be quite right and helpful for you. But because of my uniqueness that "thing" would be destructive in my life. God may say to you, "This is okay for you" and then say to me, "But Jim, you can't handle it."

If you can personally and honestly answer yes to all seven questions, then for you it is probably acceptable. However, if the Spirit points out just one no answer, then you would be violating God's Word to be involved in that particular practice or activity.

And by struggling through each principle, you will not only know *what* you believe, but also *why*. "My church says ——" will not be strong enough an argument when the pressure to conform is on. But a well-thought-through position will!

1. Is it beneficial and constructive?

"Everything is permissible" was the unofficial slogan at the church in Corinth. A quick reading of the first letter reveals how far they had taken this attitude. (Take a look at 1 Corinthians 5:1-2 and 11:17-21 before going on.)

Chapter five implies this "freedom" has led to greed, swindling, idolatry, immorality, slander, and drunkenness in the church. Paul appeals for balance! *"Everything is permissible"* – but not everything is beneficial. "Everything is permissible" – but not everything is constructive.

A few years ago "If it feels good, do it" was printed on every T-shirt, bumper sticker, schoolbag, and three-inch button in North America. A story began to make its rounds about a teen driving a tiny sportscar with the popular bumper sticker. At a stoplight, a big burly man pulls up behind the young man, goes to his trunk, pulls out a sledge hammer and casually shatters the young person's windshield.

"Ya know, son, I've always wanted to do that. And let me tell ya, it *did* feel good!"

Today the philosophy is "eat, drink, and be merry, for tomorrow we die." If you don't know God personally, it is easy to look at the nuclear arms race and political upheaval and say, "Why not!?"

But Christians are not locked in the present. God has shown us a glimpse of the future, so we are able to make choices based on long-range consequences. Even here on earth, our faith seems more practical than those who have done things that felt good at the time. But right now they have destroyed health and relationships.

Don't you know that you yourselves are God's temple and that God's Spirit lives in you? If anyone destroys God's temple, God will destroy him; for God's temple is sacred, and you are that temple (1 Corinthians 3:16-17).

Before I slip into a pair of purple sweat socks I need to ask:

Will this "thing" build me up physically? Mentally? Socially and spiritually?

What do health authorities say about it?

Will it be beneficial and constructive five years from now? Twenty years from now?

2. Is it not mastering me?

I love low-budget horror films. Especially where sinister scientists or martian mutants take control of mild-mannered humans, giant sea turtles, tomatoes or even shag carpeting. (Really, someone actually made a film called "The Attack of the Killer Tomatoes." "The Creeping Terror" featured rugged drama as carpeting threatened to devour Lake Tahoe High School.)

I guess I love the idea of manipulators finally getting justice in the end. And of course the victims always regain control of their own lives.

All of us have those areas where people or "things" are trying to control us. But there is hope! According to Galatians 5, one fruit of the Spirit is *self-*

control. And Peter warns us to *prepare your minds for action; be self-controlled; . . . As obedient children, do not conform to the evil desires you had when you lived in ignorance. But just as he who called you is holy, so be holy in all you do* (1 Peter 1:13-15).

We can be filled with His Spirit. We can be guided by His Spirit. But it is still my responsibility to be in control of my actions and attitudes.

Any time any "thing" becomes a habit and takes over that control, I am a slave to it. So we need to ask ourselves: Do purple sweat socks have the potential to control us physically? How about mentally, socially, or spiritually?

Total freedom is Christ's purpose for His followers. *If you hold to my teaching, you are really my disciples. Then you will know the truth, and the truth will set you free. . . . I tell you the truth, everyone who sins is a slave to sin. Now a slave has no permanent place in the family, but a son belongs to it forever. So if the Son sets you free, you will be free indeed* (John 8:31-32, 34-36).

Satan also promises freedom. But his brand only offers chains and shackles thinly plated with freedom. His most effective trap is to offer freedom to have legitimate needs and desires fulfilled right now.

His first victim was Eve. *"God knows that when you eat of it [the tree] your eyes will be opened, and you will be like God, knowing good and evil." When the woman saw that the fruit of the tree was good for food and pleasing to the eye, and also desirable for gaining wisdom, she took some and ate it* (Genesis 3:5-6).

That was not a *bad* desire! God had created Adam and Eve to have fellowship with Him and to become like Him. "Becoming like God" should be the goal of us all. And yet it is a lifelong, sometimes painful process. Satan offered Eve a shortcut to that desire. But you'll remember it ended in just the opposite.

Sex, pleasure, independence, and maybe even purple sweat socks are God-given desires. But Satan's shortcuts inevitably end up in slavery to habits and lifestyles that are no longer satisfying.

Christ offers temporary slavery. *If anyone would come after me, he must deny himself and take up his cross and follow me* (Mark 8:34). But that "slavery" always results in long-lasting freedom. *I have come that they may have life, and have it to the full* (John 10:10b).

Purple sweat socks are "things" and thus are "permissible." Just be sure they are also "beneficial," "constructive," and not "mastering" you.

For further reading

> 1 Corinthians 6:13-20
> Galatians 5:13-14, 22
> 1 Timothy 4:1-5

2. General principles

(3) Is it motivated by love for others? (Part 1)

Nobody should seek his own good, but the good of others (1 Corinthians 10:24).

"My name is Jimmy Watkins and I am five years old. I wanted to bring my dog Gertrude with me, but my Mommy says Gertrude is in love and cannot come out of the house for a whole week. Love must be something awful. I asked Billy Smith. He is in sixth grade and knows everything.

"Billy Smith said, 'Love makes you feel light-headed and your stomach turns flip-flops, and you feel warm all over your body.' I was in love last week and my mommy took me to the doctor and I got a shot where I sit down. And I didn't even get a lollipop.

"My Sunday school teacher taught us a song about love. It goes 'For God so loved the world, He gave . . .' Ah, 'For God so loved the world, He gave . . .' I forgot the rest. I guess love is giving. I gave Betty Green the chicken-pops and I gave Junior Jackson a black eye, but I think it just means good stuff.

"You can learn a lot about love on the TV. Like did you know that love is in the afternoon. That's what the man on TV says. And did you know that love is also chocolate pudding. Yup, the commercial says 'thanks for the love in my lunch box.' And do you know what is in the lunch box? A can of chocolate pudding! Love also tickles your nose and gives you the burpies. 'Canada Dry tastes like love!' And ginger-ale always tickles my nose and gives me the burpies.

"I also learned on TV that love can be manu-fractured. So last night I got my plastic building blocks out and I asked real nice – I even said 'please' – 'Daddy, can you help me make some love?' Daddy turned real red and said "Never say that again!' I asked Billy Smith. He is in sixth grade and just knows everything. He said that love is a four-letter word and you must never use them.

"After my daddy turned back to pink he said that I had been watching too much TV, and that God is the one who gives us real love. Daddy says it's liking somebody just the way they are. I always ride my tricy-cle past Betty Green's house without my hands to im-press her. She is in first grade and is beautiful. She even has this really neat chipped front tooth. But she just yells out the window that I'm mentally retired!

"But Mommy and Daddy love me just the way I am. Even when I got sick on the brand-new carpet. And they even loved me when I took the 'lectric hedge trimmers and gave Gertrude a haircut. (They did give me a spanking though.)

"But I know they love me just the way I am. And God loves me just the way I am. It makes me feel all warm inside, like when you come in from the snow, and your nose is dripping, and your mommy gives you a big cup of hot chocolate and it thaws your insides out. And God loves you just the way you are too!"

Hmmmmm. There *are* a lot of ideas on the subject of love. And that's frightening! Our society allows for just about any action as long as the motive is "love." In a way they're right. When Christ was asked what is the greatest commandment, His answer was love.

"Love the Lord your God with all your heart and with all your soul and with all your mind." This is the first and greatest commandment. And the second is like it: "Love your neighbor as yourself." All the Law and the Prophets hang on these two commandments" (Matthew 22:37-40).

Paul says the same thing in Romans 13:9-10. All commandments from God *are summed up in this one rule: "Love your neighbor as yourself." Love does no harm to its neighbor. Therefore love is the fulfillment of the law.*

The problem is with our definition of love. We say "I love deep-dish pizza," "I love my mother," "I love God" and we mean three very different things.

The Greeks were smart to use four different words for love in their vocabulary.

Eros: Taken from the Latin god of love, it referred to sensual or sexual love, as well as the love of things. When I say "I love deep-dish pizza, the sea breeze in my face, and my word-processor," I am really saying "I *eros* deep-dish pizza, etc."

Phileo, Storge: These words are used throughout Scripture to refer to brotherly love, love for mankind, and love for one's family. "I *phileo* the people at church," "I *storge* my kid brother," and "I *phileo* anyone who buys this book."

Agape: *Agape* isn't based on warm mushy feelings or even on a relationship. It's a willful, deliberate, I-choose-to-love-you kind of love. In Scripture, *agape* is used to describe love for the good or the evil of life. It does describe the kind of unconditional love God has for us! (Read 1 John 4:7-12 and 1 Corinthians 13 before continuing. Come on, this will make more sense after you read it!)

Judy pounded out her words with her fist on the front of my desk. "I just can't love my brother. I see all these TV shows with brothers and sisters hugging and doing things together, but I just can't work up any warm feelings for the kid. I mean, his idea of warmth and affection is to slap me on the rear and say 'love ya Sis.' If I wanted to be slapped on the rear I'd join a major league team. And that's another thing. I hate sports. But every afternoon when I'm trying to get my homework done he's out there banging that stupid basketball up and down on the sidewalk or bouncing it against the side of the house. How can I feel love when I'm about to flunk algebra?''

"Judy, don't you drive your brother to Little League each day? And don't you walk him to Sunday school each week? Didn't you say you help him with his homework most nights?''

"Yah, but what does that have to do with feeling love for him?''

"It doesn't have anything to do with feelings, but it has a lot to do with love.''

       *   *   *   *

"Look, I've never told anyone this before, but after Bobby was born I just haven't felt any love for my wife. She's always tired and the baby's always crying.'' Jack paused and stared out the office window. "I guess the love is gone between us.''

"Didn't you say you helped feed Bobby?''

"Well, I take the 2:00 in the morning feeding so she can get some sleep. She has to take care of him all the time that I'm gone to work, so I try to help with housework when I get home and take the middle-of-the-night feedings and diaper changes.''

As I talked with Judy and Jack, I discovered they had a deep love for their families. It just wasn't the type of love you'll hear on top-forty radio. But then changing diapers at 2:00 a.m. or driving your kid brother to Little League probably wouldn't make it to number one on the charts.

Paul's definition in 1 Corinthians 13 emphasizes that *agape* love is not based on feelings at all. Pupils fixed and dilated, dizziness, fever, tense abdominal muscles, lack of concentration, and increased heart rate may be the symptoms of the world's "love.'' (More than likely they're the symptoms of appendicitis!)

Agape love is actions: being kind, not boasting,

not keeping records of wrong, not being rude, protecting. *Agape* love is attitudes: patient, not envious, not proud, not self-seeking, not easily angered, rejoicing in truth – not evil, trusting, hoping, persevering.

2. General principles

(3) Is it motivated by love for others? (Part 2)

O K, but what does love have to do with wearing purple sweat socks?" You can guess by now who said that! We spent that week looking at love's direct relationship to ethical issues.

Patience

Paul's definition of love is exactly opposite the popular philosophy of existentialism. Maybe that's a new term for some of you. The first three beliefs of the existentialist are . . .
1. To exist is what a man is.
2. To exist is to realize a man can be nothing.
3. To exist is to take seriously all of one's experiences including moods as well as the rational process.
If you have a baby brother or sister, you *know* what an existentialist is! I desperately tried to reassure my daughter Faith that in just minutes I would meet her rather vocal demands for lunch. "See Daddy heat the water to warm Faith's bottle. See Daddy put the

bottle in the hot water. See Daddy scald his hand."
Paul is not any better. Even during the 30 seconds
it takes to heat his cereal in the microwave he is loudly
making his requests known.

The only thing that babies and existentialists can
be sure of is "I exist in the present situation." (Thus
"situational ethics" fits well into this philosophy.) "I'm
not sure about the future, so whatever meets my need
now is the most important."

From the oldie-goldies like "I Can't Get No Satisfaction" and "Let's Get Physical" to current hits, the
world has told us love is that frustration and yearning
for instant gratification ("If morning's echo says we've
sinned, well it was what I wanted now," or "Let the
devil take tomorrow, but tonight I need a friend.")

Psychologists, as well as God, remind us that one
sign of maturity is the ability to wait for our needs
to be met. *Agape* love is patient. It is willing to allow
a relationship time to develop. It is willing to wait for
God to resolve a conflict. It is willing to wait until
marriage for intercourse. It is willing to put the other
person's welfare above our own.

Eros, and sometimes *phileo,* is "baby" love. But
like Paul's checkpoints one and two, *agape* wants what
is best in the long run. That's why it can be patient.

Kind understanding

The term "situational ethics" gives the impression
that outward circumstances determine right and
wrong. *Eros* looks at the exterior, the physical. But
kind understanding comes from a Greek word that emphasizes the need to see below the surface. *Agape*
produces a depth of understanding of people and issues.

My seven-year-old put it well, after watching her
girl friend's crush on a seventh-grader. "I don't think
it's really love, 'cause real love doesn't make you
stupid."

The Bible agrees. *And this is my prayer: that your*

love may abound more and more in knowledge and depth of insight, so that you may be able to discern what is best . . . (Philippians 1:9-10).

Then we will no longer be infants, tossed back and forth by the waves, and blown here and there by every wind of teaching and by the cunning and craftiness of men in their deceitful scheming. Instead, speaking the truth in love, we will in all things grow up into him who is the Head, that is, Christ (Ephesians 4:14-15).

My purpose is that they may be encouraged in heart and united in love, so that they may have the full riches of complete understanding, in order that they may know the mystery of God, namely, Christ, in whom are hidden all the treasures of wisdom and knowledge. I tell you this so that no one may deceive you by fine-sounding arguments (Colossians 2:2-4).

It is God's love that gives us the ability to make sound judgments on the issues of our day! In these few verses He promises that *agape* love will provide—

1. **Knowledge and depth of insight**
2. **The ability to discern what is best**
3. **Solid answers to keep us from deception**
4. **Spiritual and mental maturity**
5. **Complete understanding, wisdom, and knowledge**
6. **The ability to see through fine-sounding arguments.**

We can have these abilities because love is our connection to God. *Dear friends, let us love one another, for love comes from God. Everyone who loves has been born of God and knows God. Whoever does not love does not know God, because God is love. This is how God showed his love among us: He sent his one and only Son into the world that we might live through him. This is love: not that we loved God, but he loved us and sent his Son as an atoning sacrifice for our sins* (1 John 4:7-10).

Just as *agape*'s love is far different from the world's, so is its wisdom. *So what about these wise men, these scholars, these brilliant debaters of this world's great affairs? God has made them all look foolish, and shown their wisdom to be useless nonsense. For God in His wisdom saw to it that the world would never find God through human brilliance, and then He stepped in and saved all those who believed His message, which the world calls foolish and silly.*

Instead, God has deliberately chosen to use ideas the world considers foolish and of little worth in order to shame those people considered by the world as wise and great (1 Corinthians 1:20-21, 27, TLB).

Does not envy

Carrie was a beautiful girl who looked like she just stepped out of *Seventeen* magazine. But as we talked she shared her frustration.

"My parents won't let me wear jeans. They keep quoting some verse about 'men's apparel,' but everybody else on campus does and it just frustrates me."

"Why do you want to wear jeans?"

"Well, ah. Everyone wears them."

"Is that all?"

"Well (long pause) I guess. I did try on a pair of my roommate's. But really, after wearing dresses all my life, they felt like they were smothering my legs."

"Then the real issue isn't jeans at all?"

"No, I guess not. I guess I just envy those who seem to have more freedom than I."

I think Asaph, in Psalm 73, felt that way too. (And who hasn't?)

Surely God is good to Israel, to those who are pure in heart. But as for me, my feet had almost slipped; I had nearly lost my foothold. For I envied the arrogant when I saw the prosperity of the wicked. They have no struggles; their bodies are healthy and strong (Psalm 73:1-4).

Asaph feels the wicked have less struggles, more money and nicer clothes. To be real honest, he wonders if it's been a waste to keep himself pure. (Ever felt that way? I have.)

It was oppressive to me till I entered the sanctuary of God; then I understood their final destiny (Psalm 73:16b-17).

When we are filled with God's love we can be content in His presence. We can be sure that each person is accountable to His divine justice. My responsibility is to live as close to Him as possible. Then I won't be envious of those around me.

Not self-seeking

Since the existentialist is sure only of his existence, all decisions are made on the basis of "what's in it for me?" They're "looking out for number one"!

Focusing on ourselves in life makes as much sense as trying to drive a car by carefully watching the dashboard. A wealth of information *is* available! The speedometer shows how fast we're going, the odometer tells how far we've gone, and the tachometer registers our rpm's. There are other wonderful dials that reveal what's happening under the hood: gauges for oil pressure, water temperature, the charging of the battery and whether the emergency brake is on.

But this constant attention to our own little world (speeding along at 55 mph) would be disastrous! We humans were designed, engineered and built to interact and affect the lives of others; not to be self-centered and constantly looking out for number one.

As we examine issues and decisions, we must ask:

How will this decision affect my family? my friends? my church? my community? my country? my world? Again, *agape* is seeking the good of others.

Does not delight in evil

If *agape* is our standard when looking at various issues, we will never be prompted to do anything outside of God's righteousness. "Love is the fulfillment of the law," so it can never violate God's written Word when taken in its proper context.

Many examples used in "values clarification" or "situational ethics" discussions deal with the "rightness" of breaking God's commandments. "Isn't there a time when lying is the loving and right thing to do?"

One situation that I hear repeatedly concerns a woman prisoner in a German POW camp. Her husband and children are safe in a neutral country. She is befriended by a guard who offers to make her pregnant so she will be released and can be reunited with her family. "Isn't adultery the loving thing to do in this situation?" God's answer is no.

Some have used the situation of Christ and His disciples picking grain along the road. Their interpretation: "It's OK to steal if you're truly hungry." The culture of the day allowed travelers to pick handfuls of grain on their journey. Farmers were even required to leave some grain in the field during harvest for the widows and the poor.

The moment we say, "Breaking a commandment is the loving thing to do," we grab the "steering wheel of our life" out of God's hands. "I can handle this situation better than you can, God" we imply.

There will be times when it will be a real struggle to keep our hands off the wheel. And yet *in all things God works for the good of those who love him, who have been called according to his purpose* (Romans 8:28). Various issues will tempt us to disobey God. But His love will always motivate us to please Him.

Rejoices in the truth

A family was having their ancestry researched and were delighted to find relatives in medicine, government, theology, law and the arts. There was only one problem: "Uncle Willie, electrocuted at the state penitentiary for armed robbery." How could they possibly include this stain on their spotless family history? They came up with this solution:

"Uncle Willie was a successful financier by age 30 and occupied a most powerful seat in the electronics field at the state's largest institution. He held this position for only a short time when he died suddenly at age 31. His death came as a great shock."

William Blake poetically warns us that truth *is* easily twisted. "A truth told with bad intent, beats all the lies one can invent." The danger of worldly thinking is its ability to sound true. The "truth" of the world *is* constantly changing. And because of this, philosophers are absolutely *sure* there is no *absolute* truth. "What is right today, may be wrong tomorrow. What is immoral today, may be the accepted norm tomorrow." These attitudes are clearly presented in PBS's study guide to the program "Hard Choices":

"There are no moral or ethical laws . . . no absolute guiding principles for human society. . . . We should feel free to adapt our morality to new social situations. As a result, ethical choices are likely to become more difficult, not because people are less moral, but because they are unable to justify their choices with fairy tales."

This kind of thinking reminds me of my wife's performing white rat. One clinical psychology project was to train a rodent to roll over. The theory was simple enough – each time the rat comes close to rolling over, toss him a food pellet. (And to ensure the rat's attention, he wasn't fed for 24 hours.) The rat realizes, "Hey, I get food when I lie down." Then, "Wow, I really get fed when I lie on my side. I wonder what will happen if I roll over?"

Lois claims she was given a rat with an extremely low brain cell count. The professor claimed she had been inconsistent in rewarding its behaviors. The tragic result was "experimental psychosis" – a rat totally confused as to what was the right or wrong response. Finally it did roll over with its little pink feet straight up – permanently – dead from stress and exhaustion.

In love, God has revealed the right behavior that will lead to a life that is filled with purpose, direction and joy. But millions of teens and adults reject God's principles and find themselves stricken with the despair and frustration of experimental psychosis.

God's love provides solid reference points on which we can firmly establish our values and beliefs.

Protects

You can always tell when a guy is in love; he wants to protect that special girl. He opens car doors to protect those dainty hands from callouses. He very carefully protects her back from flying objects with his arm around her. He protects her little toes by carrying her over mud puddles. Love protects! Somehow we must carry that protective nature of first love into each situation.

And I'm protective when it comes to seat belts. The car doesn't move until Lois, Faith and Paul are safely strapped in. While I was buckling the kids in, a huge bee flew in the car door. Faith and Paul were terrified as I heroically chased it out of the car with my bare hands. On the way home my daughter announced, "If a bee bites you, you'll turn into a 'killer bee'!"

"Who told you that dumb story?"

There was silence for a moment, then she sobbed, "I made it up. I was just trying to be funny."

I want my family to have the protection of seat belts. I risk personal safety to battle "killer bees." Every night I make sure all the windows and doors are locked. We never leave Paul and Faith alone. Yet while they are safe physically, their fragile egos and self-concepts can be shattered by words.

Agape is protective. As we judge issues, we need to ask:

Is this particular issue taking into consideration the rights of the weak? the unprotected? the vulnerable? the defenseless? and the needy around me?

This love and wisdom from God, however, does not come in a lump sum at conversion. It grows and develops right up to the day we meet St. Peter. He encourages us in his second letter to *make every effort to add to your faith goodness; and to goodness, knowledge; and to knowledge, self-control; and to self-control, perseverance; and to perseverance, godliness; and to godliness, brotherly kindness; and to brotherly kindness, love. For if you possess these qualities in increasing measure, they will keep you from being ineffective and unproductive in your knowledge of our Lord Jesus Christ* (2 Peter 1:5-8).

On our first trip to the altar, we are given the *quality* of God's love and knowledge. It is then our responsibility to live in close relationship to God so it may increase in *quantity*. When I was in second grade my family made their first trip to Florida. While we passed through Georgia I was fascinated with the bright red clay. Excitedly I dug into the strange soil with a paper cup and proudly kept it in my room for the next several years.

I had the quality of Georgia red clay in that beat-up paper cup. It probably contained pollen from orange and peach blossoms, pulverized rock, orchard fertilizer, and a host of other microscopic particles that an expert could identify as Georgia red clay. I had the quality, but not the quantity. (I wanted to bring home more, but Mom and Dad frowned upon filling the trunk up with the delightful dirt.)

"New born" Christians have the same *quality* of God's love and knowledge that a "faithful saint of the church" has. The difference is a lifetime of commitment to Christ, prayer, Bible study, and fellowship that increased the *quantity*. God will increase your wisdom and discernment as you increase in your love for Him and others. *Agape* love needs to be central as you work out your position on each issue.

Nobody should seek his own good, but the good of others (1 Corinthians 10:24).

For further reading . . .

Matthew 5:38-48
Romans 12:9-21
1 John 3:16-18
Revelation 2:1-6

Say It With Love by Howard Hendricks (Victor Books)
Perfect Love by Keith Drury, David Holdren, Jimmy
  Johnson, David Keith, Blair Ritchey, James Wat-
  kins and Dick Wynn (Wesley Press)

2. General principles

(4) Is it producing a clear conscience?
(5) Is it not causing a weaker Christian to sin?

*E*at anything sold in the meat market without raising questions of conscience, for, "The earth is the Lord's, and everything in it."

If some unbeliever invites you to a meal and you want to go, eat whatever is put before you without raising questions of conscience. But if anyone says to you, "This has been offered in sacrifice," then do not eat it, both for the sake of the man who told you and for conscience' sake – the other man's conscience, I mean, not yours. For why should my freedom be judged by another's conscience? If I take part in the meal with thankfulness, why am I denounced because of something I thank God for?

Do not cause anyone to stumble, whether Jews, Greeks or the church of God (1 Corinthians 10:25-30, 32).

You may know that there is nothing wrong with what you do, even from God's point of view, but keep it to yourself; don't flaunt your faith in front of others who might be hurt by it. In this situation, happy is

*the man who does not sin by doing what he knows
is right. But anyone who believes that something he
wants to do is wrong shouldn't do it. He sins if he
does, for he thinks it is wrong, and so for him it is
wrong. Anything that is done apart from what he feels
is right is sin* (Romans 14:22-23, TLB).

4. Is it producing a clear conscience?

The college students called her "Rodent" behind
her back. I'm not sure if many even knew her real
name. The tiny and frail girl always wore black dresses,
never shaved her legs and only occasionally washed
her hair. It was tightly braided and piled on top, so
with some imagination it *did* appear mouse-like.

I began to ask friends about this girl. She had
surprised her parents with her arrival while they were
in their fifties, and had been brought up in a church
which had preached exclusively about "things."

"Lois, her suite-mates ought to kidnap her, wash
and set her hair, shave her legs, and haul her off to
a Mary Kay Cosmetics party."

"She would feel so guilty, it might just destroy
what faith she has," my wife-to-be answered.

Several years later, I returned to campus as assis-
tant pastor at the college church. I met many students
struggling with that same kind of guilt. In the freedom
of being away from home, many had done things they
had been taught were wrong. Now they were filled
with incredible guilt and shame.

Usually the "sin" was something the Bible mentioned nothing about, but I remembered Lois's warning. Even if the hang-up was totally irrational, there
still was no way around God's Word – "No one can
innocently do what he believes is sin."

God does not want us to be slaves to past hang-
ups and unfair peer pressure. Nor does He want us
to be filled with guilt feelings, confusion, fears, and
doubts by doing something we feel is wrong. Both ap-
proaches are disastrous.

The secret I found was to have each sort through

their feelings. What guilt was from God and what guilt was from human peer pressure and past training? (There is danger in preaching human opinions tightly woven around biblical truth. It becomes difficult for many to separate the strands. And many at college tossed out the whole ball of yarn – both rigid man-made rules and their relationship with God.)

Paul makes this distinction between humanly produced remorse and godly conviction:

Your sorrow led you to repentance. For you became sorrowful as God intended and so were not harmed in any way by us. Godly sorrow brings repentance that leads to salvation and leaves no regret, but worldly sorrow brings death (2 Corinthians 7:9b-10).

Psychologists claim our upbringing produces two "accusers" – the "Ideal Self" (our ideas and our parents' expectations of what we should be) and the "Punitive Self" (a "little parent" still within us shaking its finger when we don't measure up to our "Ideal Self").

Any time we violate the "Ideal Self," the "Punitive Self" begins to tell us "We're no good," "People will be disappointed in us," "We are a 'wretch' and a 'worm,' " "God won't love us if we act like that."

But God never makes a Christian feel guilty. It is Satan who is our accuser (Revelation 12:10) and God who is our Advocate (1 John 2:1). Paul writes, *Who will bring any charge against those whom God has chosen? It is God who justifies* (Romans 8:33).

When the great reformer Martin Luther experienced feelings of overwhelming guilt he would reply, "Go ahead, Mr. Law, and accuse me as much as you like, I know I have committed many sins. But that doesn't bother me. You have got to shout louder, Mr. Law. I am deaf you know. Talk as much as you like, I am dead to you .. . . My conscience is a lady and a queen and has nothing to do with the likes of you, because my conscience lives to Christ under another law, a new and better law, the law of grace."

Once we have realized that guilt feelings come from a variety of "accusers," not from God, does that mean we are free to sin as often as we please with no guilt or remorse? No! As Paul writes, "Worldly sorrow" (the "Ideal Self," the "Punitive Self" and Satan) leads to death, but "godly sorrow" leads to loving conformity to God's will. God does make us aware of sinful attitudes and actions, but it is very different from what we often call a "guilty conscience."

Bruce Narramore and Bill Count, in *Freedom From Guilt,* make these distinctions . . .

	Psychological Guilt	Constructive Guilt
Person in primary focus	Your self	God or others
Attitudes or actions in primary focus	Past misdeeds	Damage done to others or our future correct deeds.
Motivation for change (if any)	To avoid feeling bad (guilt feelings)	To help others, to promote our growth, or to do God's will (love feelings)
Attitude toward self	Anger and frustration	Love and respect combined with concern
Result	a) External change (for improper motivations) b) Stagnation due to paralyzing effect of guilt c) Further rebellion	Repentance and change based on an attitude of love, mutual respect

Even more important than reading a good book on the subject, is to talk to someone you trust about these feelings. Becoming aware of the causes of "false guilt" and becoming sensitive to God's loving correction are keys to success.

It may require weeks or months to sort through your feelings. During this time, the principle must still remain, "Even if I know this is an irrational hang-up and there are no biblical grounds for it, I will not do it if it produces tension, mental stress or a cloudy conscience."

5. Is it *not* causing a *weaker* Christian to sin?

The rest of 1 Corinthians 8 provides another principle. **(STOP!** Do not go beyond this point before reading 1 Corinthians 8:7-13 and Matthew 18:6-8.)

Remember, one of the hottest issues was "Should a Christian eat meat that had been offered to idols?" Each day in the heathen temples, satanic priests placed meat on an altar before their gods. Then at the end of the ceremony, the beef was sold at the temple restaurant at a reduced price.

Some Christians believed it was good stewardship of the Lord's money to buy steaks at a bargain price. But other equally sincere Christians believed it was wrong to buy it, since it was associated with the immoral worship of Satan. They were also concerned that their association with the idol temple might lead new converts back into the occult. (Remember almost all the early Christians had been involved with idols and pagan worship, before accepting Christ as Lord.)

Does this mean we have to live up to every other person's convictions? Look at the verses again. Both Paul and Christ address our actions to—

the weak
anyone with a weak conscience
weak brother
little ones.

They are speaking of new or young believers, not of Sister Smith who's been a Christian eighty-five years, and prefers pink to purple. We are not bound to her tastes, convictions, or values. But we must be careful that our actions don't—

become a stumbling block
cause her to be spiritually *destroyed by our knowledge*
wound [her] weak conscience
cause [her] to fall into sin
cause [her] to fall
cause one who believes in me to sin

Her dislike of the color purple won't cause her to give up her relationship with God. If Sister Smith prefers slower music than the teen choir sings, it may offend her aesthetic tastes, but I doubt if it will cause her spiritual damage.

I also need to be careful, though, that I'm not doing something that bugs Sister Smith, just to bug her. (If that's the case, I need to reread the chapter on love!)

William Barclay, in *The Daily Study Bible,* gives us this final thought. "No man has any right to claim a right, to indulge in a pleasure, (or) to demand a liberty which may be the ruination of someone else. It may be that he has the strength of mind and will to keep that pleasure in its proper place; it may be that that course of action is safe enough for him; but he has not only himself to think about; he must think of the weaker brother. A pleasure or an indulgence which may be the ruin of someone else is not a pleasure but a sin."

For further reading . . .

Romans 14:13-15, 20-23

Freedom From Guilt by Bruce Narramore and Bill Counts (Harvest House)

2. General principles

(6) Is it a glory to God?
(7) Is it good for my witness?

Why do we really want to wear purple sweat socks? Purple is our favorite color? All our friends wear them? The TV says we need to? They are our only clean pair? A good friend gave them to us and we don't want to hurt her feelings by not wearing them?

There may be several different reasons for doing one thing. And so Paul's last two principles deal with motives.

So whether you eat or drink or whatever you do, do it all for the glory of God. . . . I try to please everybody in every way. For I am not seeking my own good but the good of many, so that they may be saved (1 Corinthians 10:31, 33b).

6. Is it a glory to God?

Just what does Paul mean here? Let's look at some ways to decide if a particular issue, action, or cause is truly glorifying God.

(1) Does it value, protect and benefit God's creation?

According to Romans 1, *God's invisible qualities – his eternal power and divine nature – have been clearly seen, being understood from what has been made* (Romans 1:20). When we devalue, destroy or endanger God's creation, we are harming those things that God uses to reveal himself to mankind.

This doesn't mean that God and His creation are one. It does mean that humans are unique creations of God, and that Christians are *temples of the Holy Spirit.*

It doesn't imply we ought to worship nature, but does mean *the earth is the Lord's and everything in it.* Everything was created by God – even the atomic particles scientists use to make "man-made elements."

This is why I've been known to "get blessed" while watching NOVA and *National Geographic* specials. I marvel at the genius of our Creator in the intricate designs, mechanisms and instincts of each creation. Even though Biology 101 was taught by an atheist, the class still increased my awe and wonder of God.

My actions on an issue must reflect my respect for God's creation. He has created it to reveal himself to a lost world.

(2) Does it promote excellence?

I'm also inspired while watching championship ice skating, track, diving, or gymnastics. Here are God's creations performing at peak skill and coordination. That's why I think Paul would have made a great Olympics coach. He stresses God's desire for us to "think on those things that are excellent and praiseworthy."

Unfortunately, many in the church don't have that Olympic drive for excellence. In fact, human effort is sometimes looked down on. I asked composer and pianist Otis Skillings about the attitude that says: "It's not the quality, but the spirit that counts."

He said, "In the last chapter of Galatians, God says, 'Do the very best job you possibly can do.' I've heard choir directors say, after running through a song once or twice, 'That's good enough for church.' That's terrible! I think it's almost a sin when singers and directors are content to sluff off and not give Him the very best. We need to work like a dog to make it the best we can.

"The verse goes on to say 'then don't compare yourself to someone else.' That's important. If we've done our best we shouldn't compare our choir with a recording group or the choir down the street."

Just "getting by" doesn't glorify God at church, school, home, work – or anyplace else. Make sure your involvement in an issue will bring out the best in you and allow you to develop and improve your talents and abilities.

The greatest challenge in life is not sorting out bad from good, but good from best! (Underline that concept in this book and in your heart.)

(3) Does it draw attention to God or strictly to self?

I haven't cried at a film since third grade when Bambi's mother died. But *Chariots of Fire* broke my long-standing record. Eric Liddle's sister is against delaying his missionary call to China to run in the 1924 Olympics. And yet Eric feels that his running and refusal to compete on Sunday will bring glory to God. His father encourages the athlete to "run in God's name and let the world stand back and wonder."

And he wins! Eric's faith and commitment brought glory to his God. So did the film's Academy Award for Best Picture in 1981.

A teen wrote me recently about this issue of glorifying God in each area of life:

Dear Pastor Jim,

I love dancing and I'm pretty good at it. I'm even taking classes to train to be a "Solid Gold" or "Fame" dancer. People in my church say that "Solid Gold" dancing is sensual and a Christian has no business doing it. Is it really bad? When I'm dancing that way it looks sensual but I don't feel that way. When I dance I become one with the music — just feeling free, not sensual.

I'm a Christian and I hate doing bad things, so please tell me, is it bad to dance like that?

R. F.

(Youth leader, notice that the church's beliefs have *not* changed his opinion. That's why it's so important to allow teens and young adults to work through the issue on their own. It is tempting to point out that many modern dances are erotic, sensual and mimic the movements of intercourse. But notice that R. F. avoids these considerations by claiming "it looks sensual, but I don't feel that way.")

I asked him to prayerfully and honestly answer these questions based on 1 Corinthians 10:

1. Am I dancing for God's glory or my own?
2. Will my performance, "which looks sensual," direct attention to God or will it arouse sensual thoughts in my audience?
3. Will my dancing be an avenue for sharing my faith?

The ball was now in *his* court. He had to come to grips with the motivation and results of his dancing.

I've had to ask myself how many of my activities (appointments, meetings, sports events, concerts, TV shows) actually glorify God. In Colossians 2, Paul says our eating and drinking, our religious festivals (carry-in dinners and church softball play-offs?) and Sabbaths are merely a shadow of Christ.

So I must ask myself, does the hustle and bustle in the church or youth group really glorify the Head of the Church? And do purple sweat socks meet St. Paul's sixth requirement?

7. Is it good for my witness?

Witnessing is not limited to knocking on doors and sharing "The Four Spiritual Laws." Our entire lifestyle of opinions, values, attitudes and actions is our witness.

No one lights a lamp and hides it in a jar or puts it under a bed. Instead, he puts it on a stand, so that those who come in can see the light. For there is nothing hidden that will not be disclosed, and nothing concealed that will not be known or brought out into the open (Luke 8:16-17).

We try to live in such a way that no one will ever be offended or kept back from finding the Lord by the way we act, so that no one can find fault with us and blame it on the Lord (2 Corinthians 6:3, *TLB*).

Unbelievers are watching our every action and reaction! Even in their disobedience or indifference, they do seem to have some high standards for those who claim to believe. Take Mrs. Jones for example. She was one of the sweetest ladies at my cousin's church. If you needed an answer to prayer, you went to this woman with the direct connection to God.

But suddenly this Christian lady began receiving very unchristian and very unladylike phone calls. Strange men started showing up at her house trailer at all hours of the night. Her neighbors began to avoid her and talk behind her back. She mentioned these strange events to my cousin.

"This sounds silly, but it seemed to begin after I changed my porch light. The store was all out of those yellow bug lights so I bought a red one."

We need to be careful what kind of "light" we are shining to our friends and neighbors. There are certain activities that even the most sinful, feel Christians shouldn't do. Some of these stereotypes may be accurate, and some may be irrational.

For instance, our youth group was planning a working trip to an Indian mission in the west. Ten teens were excited about paying their own way to paint buildings and help around the compound – until we received a letter from the director.

"The Indians we are working with have the stereotype that all Christians dress conservatively and have short hair. Apparently this is the result of missionaries of the past who dwelled on externals. While we do not hold these beliefs, to effectively minister to the Indians here you'll need to ask all your girls to wear dresses and the boys to have fairly short hair."

Suddenly interest dropped to two. "I'm not getting a haircut for somebody's idea of what a Christian is supposed to look like!"

We did go – with just two. And my barber did come up with an all-things-to-all-people haircut. By combing it back over my ears it gave the illusion of being very short for the Indians, and by combing it straight down it allowed me to relate to the youth group back home. And we were able to reach several of the Indians with the good news of Christ.

I do need to be conscious of my reputation so I might be more effective in sharing my faith. Am I viewed by non-Christians as honest, sincere, ethical, well-informed, and loving? And more specifically: Are purple sweat socks helping or hurting my witness?

For further reading . . .

Romans 14:16-18
Matthew 25:14-30

3. Does God change His mind?

Do they have a 'Part Two' of this, Pastor Jim?"

"Ah, no, that's all there is. You say you read the entire Bible this week?"

"Yah, it's good stuff, but God sure changes His mind a lot, doesn't He?"

Stan was a week-old Christian, but he was already asking some difficult questions. As we try to understand God's perspective on issues, we too may wonder "God sure changes His mind a lot, doesn't He?"

1. Scripture does *appear* to contradict itself.

I could never understand girls in grade school. They never did anything interesting during recess. They jumped rope, but mostly they just stood around giggling. And they dressed Barbie dolls when they could have been throwing rocks at pop cans, or hanging by one knee from atop the monkey bars.

I could never understand girls in junior high. They never did anything interesting during lunch break.

They just stood around giggling. (Not even any jump rope or Barbie dolls!)

But then I discovered "Karen." She didn't play football or even have a dirt bike, but there was this strange attraction. I found myself plotting ways to get to sit next to her on the bus. I was ecstatic when I found out we had three classes together.

But I also began to discover how different girls were from guys. There must be something more than the charts in Health Class. These gorgeous creatures were a confusing blend of contradictions.

Finally in literature class we read an Indian folk tale that confirmed my suspicions. According to the myth, God had run out of solid materials when it came to making woman. So He looked around and took . . .

> the fearfulness of a rabbit and the vanity of a
> peacock,
> the softness of a bird's breast and the hardness
> of a diamond,
> the sweetness of honey and the cruelty of a tiger,
> the burning of fire and the coldness of deep snow,
> the talkativeness of a magpie and the singing of
> a nightingale,
> the falseness of a crane and the faithfulness of
> a mother lion.

And from these elements the Creator gave Adam his wife. Suddenly all the girls between Karen and my one and only, Lois, were less frustrating. (Not less confusing, but less frustrating!) They were supposed to be beyond my male logic! It all made perfect sense to them; I just couldn't see the connection between the apparent contradictions.

I could never understand God in grade school. "Why didn't He answer my prayers for a pony like the promise verses said?"

I could never understand God in junior high. "Why did God tell the Israelites to kill every man, woman, child, and all the cattle when Jesus told us to love our enemies?"

I could never understand God in high school.

"How could God be Father, Son, and Holy Ghost, and yet be one? How could Jesus be 100% God and 100% man?" "How can we have absolute free will when God has absolute control?"

I've discovered my biggest mistake was looking at God and girls from only one viewpoint. The Bible does *appear* to contradict itself. The God of the Old Testament *seems* to be opposite of the God of the New.

But it is like the three blind men who came upon an elephant. Grabbing his trunk, the first man announced, "An elephant is like a fire hose." Grasping his tail, the second challenged, "No, an elephant is like a piece of rope." "Wrong!" the third shouted, bumping into its leg. "An elephant is like a tree trunk."

God is too big and too complex to fit into our limited logic. We can only see various "sides" of God, but we can't see the invisible connections that make Him a whole unit.

God is *not* unreasonable, illogical, or inconsistent. He is the same today as He was 2,000 years ago or 6,000 years ago. We are merely seeing various "sides" of an incredibly complex Being.

> *He is compassionate, He is angry;*
> *He is forgiving, He is judgmental;*
> *He is comforting, He is fearful;*
> *He is healing, He is destructive;*
> *He is convicting souls, He is hardening hearts;*
> *He is allowing each free will, He is in control;*
> *He is loving sinners, He is hating sin;*
> *He is called a lamb, He is called a lion;*
> *He is the Good Shepherd, He is the King of Kings.*

False religions and cults evolve when men ignore those "sides" that won't fit into their human logic. Many have become rigid legalists by accepting only the judgmental side of God. Many more have become careless in their life and morals, feeling "a loving God would never send anyone to eternal punishment."

We need to see all "sides" of God. Even though

they may *seem* opposite in our finite reasoning, remember God sees the connection between the two.

Could it be that God gave us the wonderfully complex female to help us understand His wonderfully complex personality? I'll never fully understand God – or my wife, but I love them dearly. And both have infinitely enriched my life!

2. Scripture was written during a different culture

You think some scripture is difficult to understand? The Apostle Peter had the same problem with Paul's letters. *His letters contain some things that are hard to understand, which ignorant and unstable people distort, as they do the other Scriptures, to their own destruction* (2 Peter 3:16).

My brother and I loved to eavesdrop on our parents' phone conversations. We could hear only one side of the conversation, but our incredibly creative little minds were eager to fill in the blanks.

"It's a secret agent. I always thought Mom worked for the CIA!"

"Yah, and I bet that foreign doctor she sees is her contact."

By using a little imagination, we had her talking to the President, James Bond, and talk-show hosts.

With the Epistles (letters) we are also listening in on one side of a conversation. We can't be sure what situations prompted certain passages. We can only guess the events that surrounded the response. By knowing something of the culture (that means actually listening during World History class), certain passages make more sense, though.

The Roman Empire dominated the majority of Bible lands during the time of Christ and the early church. Some estimate that because of this almost half of the population were slaves. This would help us understand the passages that remind "slaves to be obedient to their masters." Scripture in no way condones slavery, but addresses the harsh reality of that time.

Slaves were usually well-educated teachers,

scribes, and craftsmen taken captive during Roman expansion. As a result, the middle class was effectively eliminated – cheap "foreign labor" had forced the "blue collar" worker out of business. Only the very rich, and the very poor existed in the civilized world at the time. Thus the New Testament emphasis on looking out for the poor, supporting widows, and the apparent harsh treatment of the rich.

Paul's warning, in 1 Corinthians 7, to avoid marriage makes sense during a period of brutal persecution of Christians. Because of the church's refusal to worship Caesar, their property was confiscated, families enslaved, and many killed for public entertainment. Not a good time to get married!

Paul's negative comments about women teaching in church, seem to make more sense when we realize that only boys were allowed any kind of formal education. Most were tutored by slaves in reading, writing, and Greek/Latin literature.

Commentaries and Bible study books will help you understand the events surrounding particular portions of Scripture. These need to be carefully and prayerfully considered before a firm conclusion is drawn.

3. Scripture teaches both law and grace.

"How much of the Old Testament are we required to obey?" was one of the hot issues debated in A.D. 40 youth groups and Sunday school classes.

The Jewish nation had not only been given the moral law (The Ten Commandments), but "covenant laws" that set them apart from their enemies. These "set apart" areas included circumcision; pure foods; special days, weeks, years, and feasts; health and hygiene regulations; and temple symbolism.

The Israelites had also been given a very special system for sacrificing perfect lambs, doves, and bulls to take the place of their guilt for disobeying God. By the priests and the sacrificial system, the Israelites were forgiven by God with the shedding of animal blood.

Christ has proclaimed, *Do not think I have come to abolish the Law or the Prophets; I have not come to abolish them but to fulfill them. I tell you the truth, until heaven and earth disappear, not the smallest letter, not the least stroke of a pen, will by any means disappear from the Law until everything is accomplished* (Matthew 5:17-18).

And so arguments for and against circumcision, pros and cons for eating meat offered to idols and other regulations, consumed much time in church board meetings and carry-in dinners.

God's moral law is *still* in effect. The punishment for sin is *still* death. But, while we can't keep the entire law, Christ fulfilled those requirements for us. He is now our "high priest" who *meets our need – one who is holy, blameless, pure, set apart from sinners, exalted above the heavens. Unlike the other high priests, he does not need to offer sacrifices day after day, first for his own sins, and then for the sins of the people. He sacrificed for their sins once for all when he offered himself* (Hebrews 7:26-27).

All the sacrificial laws and requirements were perfectly *fulfilled* in Christ's holy, blameless, pure sacrifice of himself. The priestly office is now done away with as Christ speaks to God in our behalf.

Therefore, there is now no condemnation for those who are in Christ Jesus, because through Christ Jesus the law of the Spirit of life set me free from the law of sin and death. For what the law was powerless to do . . . God did by sending his own Son . . . in order that the righteous requirements of the law might be fully met in us (Romans 8:1-4).

What shall we say, then? Is the law sin? Certainly not! Indeed I would not have known what sin was except through the law. For I would not have known what coveting really was if the law had not said "Do not covet" (Romans 7:7). The law doesn't make anyone righteous by following it – it points out our rebellion.

He forgave us all our sins, having canceled the written code, with its regulations, that was against us and that stood opposed to us; he took it away,

nailing it to the cross. And having disarmed the pow-
ers and authorities, he made a public spectacle of
them, triumphing over them by the cross.

Therefore do not let anyone judge you by what
you eat or drink, or with regard to a religious festival,
a New Moon celebration or a Sabbath day. These are
a shadow of the things that were to come; the reality,
however, is found in Christ (Colossians 2:13b-17).

My parents faced a weekly battle to get me ready
for church. The ritual began on Saturday: "Shine your
shoes before you watch TV." Sunday morning followed
with protests against taking a bath, brushing my teeth,
wearing a clip-on tie, and producing a high-gloss shine
on my hair with Brylcream.

Then I discovered Patti. The battle continued, but
on a different front.

"How much longer are you going to be in that
tub?"

"Who used up all the toothpaste and Brylcream?"

"Jim, did you borrow my new tie again?"

Love had replaced the "law" in producing the de-
sired effect.

The commandments, "Do not commit adultery,"
"Do not murder," "Do not steal," "Do not covet," and
whatever other commandment there may be, are
summed up in this one rule: "Love your neighbor as
yourself." Love does no harm to its neighbor. Therefore
love is the fulfillment of the law (Romans 13:9-10).

As we look for insights into the issues, we need
to be careful to take scripture in the context of the
whole and to view it from the perspective of the culture
at the time.

The Bible is absolutely clear on the absolute essentials of salvation:

God loves us.

All have sinned.

The wages of sin is death.

Christ is God.

He died and rose again to take the punishment
for our sins.

Because of this, we can personally know God the

Father and be energized by His Spirit for pure living.

Anyone can understand these concepts. But some passages are so obscure no one can understand them. Anyone who claims to know their absolute meaning is ignorant of the issue or has a tremendous ego to believe he is smarter or holier than 2,000 years' worth of puzzled experts.

Fortunately these very few verses aren't necessary to understand that the rigid and legalistic "law" has been fulfilled in Christ, and replaced with the "law of love."

For further reading . . .

1 Timothy 1:8-11
Hebrews 9:1–10:25

God, I Don't Understand by Kenneth Boa (Victor Books)

III. What does God's Spirit say about purple sweat socks?

1. How can I hear God's Spirit?

I can't see where we're going!'' Headlights of on-coming cars blurred into an eerie glow as Dave cautiously inched off the road.

"I'll scrape it off," I offered, venturing into the freezing rain and slush. But three blocks later the windshield was once again iced over. And once again, back into the storm for more scraping and shivering.

During the moments the '67 VW was actually moving, Dave and I reviewed the Bible study we had just come from.

"I know the frustration John was talking about. It is hard trying to find God's will. Remember third-grade Sunday school when Mrs. Conrad told the story of Moses and the burning bush? I spent the whole afternoon sitting on the back steps waiting for the spirea bush to burst into flames and this booming voice to come out saying 'James Norman Watkins! Take off thy Nikes and come forth. For behold I have something important to tell thee!' "

"Yah, and the next week was about God talking

from the smoke and fire from Mount Sinai. Didn't you say you spent the week peering into the trash burner waiting for God to say something?"

"I'm afraid so, Dave. I guess the most frustrating thing is hearing the older people say, 'God spoke to me about – whatever.' I've knelt by my bed, tried to quiet my mind, and said, 'God, I'm trying to figure out if this thing is right or wrong. Please tell me.' "

"And absolutely nothing happens, right?"

"Yah, you don't get any answers either!?"

By this time the windshield was coated once more.

"Hey, Dave, it's actually starting to defrost a spot on my side!" I moved some gloves, a ten-year-old road map, and a paperback book to peer out the hole. "Tell you what. You run the gas and brakes from your side, and I'll steer from over here."

"Well – I guess it's that or spend the rest of our lives on Capital Avenue. Tell me when we come to red lights and curves and pedestrians and stuff!"

"Trust me, Dave! And make sure you listen well!"

Obviously, we arrived alive or there would be another person's name on the front of this book. But lying in bed, my mind floated from our questions about "hearing God" to our daring ride in the sleet. We had been searching for "signs," "fleeces," "omens," "visions," or "dreams" that would give us some inkling of God's thoughts on various issues and decisions two freshmen in college needed. Maybe it was just like our ride home in Dave's VW!

1. Give God the "steering wheel" of your life.

Therefore, I urge you, brothers, in view of God's mercy, to offer your bodies as living sacrifices, holy and pleasing to God – this is your spiritual act of worship. Do not conform any longer to the pattern of this world, but be transformed by the renewing of your mind. Then you will be able to test and approve what God's will is – his good, pleasing, and perfect will (Romans 12:1-2).

I had not fully trusted the control of my life to God. Sure, I had given Him the radio, the glove compartment, and the back seat of my life. But I had never willfully turned over the steering wheel. I had been driving blindly down the road of life, when God wanted to give me meaning and purpose to my journey. He was in the car, but I didn't trust Him steering.

Chad and I borrowed his folks' brand-new T-Bird, splashed on half a bottle of after-shave, and headed to the big game to meet some girls. As we approached a traffic light, a car that looked as if Fred Flintstone had traded it in had died in the intersection. We spun around it, squealed our tires and headed on down the street.

Suddenly "Fred" began gaining on us, then pulled up beside us. His face was scarred and his eyes peered out of deep sockets. "He's a late-night-show ax murderer!" Chad stomped the accelerator. But the faster we drove, the faster he chased, constantly glaring at us. Out of the corner of my eye I saw him pull something chrome-plated out of the glove compartment.

"He's got a gun, Chad!" I tried to pull Chad down onto the floorboard with me, as he tried to regain control of the speeding car. Then the worse happened . . . a badge waved from our pursuer's window.

This was my *second* experience with the Battle Creek Township Police. One bright summer day, my brother and I decided to let our guinea pigs breathe some fresh air. We were having a great time as they scurried in the grass – until both spied a hole in our cement block garage. And being the clever guinea pigs they were, they pushed a cement chip into the hole behind them.

What does a mom do when her five- and eight-year-olds are crying hysterically, her husband is at work, and two guinea pigs are holed up in the garage? She calls the Battle Creek Township Police!

That black-and-white car was the most beautiful sight I had ever seen. I knew help had arrived, and they would save "Hamilette" and "Squeaky" from certain death.

There was a big difference in my two reactions to the local police. In one case, I knew help had arrived. In the second, I "knew" Chad and I were on our way to glory. The difference was *knowing* the police.

I had asked Christ into my life in second grade, while hiding under my rolltop desk during a lightning storm. He was in my life; I hadn't given Him control of my life. I just knew if I did, He would make me be a missionary to some place with lots of snakes and a menu of grubs and raw fish.

But through the gift of a *Living Bible*, I began to know God. I discovered He wanted the "steering wheel of my life," not to manipulate or enslave me, but to give me meaningful direction. It wasn't until I really knew of His unconditional love, that I could trust Him with the decisions of my life.

The first step, then, in understanding God's thoughts, is to present yourself a "living sacrifice." Dick Wynn, the president of Youth For Christ, has one of the best definitions of this total commitment.

"It is giving all you know about yourself, to all you know about God."

All my talents, abilities, dreams, and aspirations are now to be used for God's glory.

2. Clear out the clutter.

Before I was able to steer Dave's car, I had to clear off the dash. Before God can direct our thoughts, we have to clear out the clutter that gets in the way of our relationship.

We are told to *not conform any longer to the pattern of this world.* In Galatians chapter five, Paul lists some characteristics of this conformity. *Sexual immorality, impurity and debauchery; idolatry and witchcraft; hatred, discord, jealousy, fits of rage, selfish ambition, dissensions, factions and envy; drunkenness, orgies, and the like* (Galatians 5:19b-21a).

Right between the "big sins" are those that we rarely hear preached against. And yet they are as deadly to our spiritual walk as any of the others.

Without a clean break from the world's values and beliefs we remain spiritually insensitive. Read the story of Balaam in Numbers chapter eleven. Here is a man to whom God verbally speaks. And yet as soon as Balaam disobeys, his donkey has more spiritual insight than he does. It is the beast of burden who sees the angel!

The story of Balaam illustrates the warning in Romans 1:21-22. *For although they knew God, they neither glorified him as God nor gave thanks to him, but their thinking became futile and their foolish hearts were darkened. Although they claimed to be wise, they became fools.*

But God doesn't leave us there. He promises to transform us by the *renewing of our minds.* And He is even aware that it is difficult to keep our minds pure when we are bombarded with dirty jokes in the locker room, with sexual advertising, sensual song lyrics, revealing fashions, and immoral behavior on TV.

The peace of God, which transcends all understanding, will guard your hearts [emotions] and your minds in Christ Jesus (Philippians 4:7).

He has promised to help us keep our minds pure, but only if we obey the next verse. *Finally, brothers, whatever is true, whatever is noble, whatever is right, whatever is pure, whatever is lovely [motivates one toward love], whatever is admirable – if anything is excellent or praiseworthy – think about such things* (Philippians 4:8).

Psychologists tell us our mind will store information for only a few seconds. This could create serious problems – never being able to remember where you lived, which restroom to use, who you were married to. But it is also a blessing – impure input will be completely forgotten in a few seconds.

The only way information is placed into permanent storage is by "rehearsal" or dwelling on it. If we do not think about that joke, or advertisement, or picture, it will not affect our attitudes or actions. If we continue to think about it, it will.

This is why Paul gives us these seven criteria for what we dwell on. Take a look at the magazines, books, TV programs, records, and movies you allow into your mind. They may be blocking out God's thoughts. God can also work to *transform* the information already stored in our mind! But we need to do our part.

3. Listen to God's instructions.

Dave paid very close attention to my shouts of "red light," "slow up for that curve" or "OK, the light's green."

But how do we "hear" God? The surest way is to get into His Word. Probably three-fourths of those decisions we need to make have either specific or general answers in Scripture.

And God speaks through other Spirit-sensitive believers. At times we may be too emotionally close to the issue to sense, without a doubt, the Lord's direction.

My wife and I felt that God was calling us into traveling evangelism work. But a good friend at our denominational headquarters advised us to find some kind of part-time work to fill the gaps in our schedule. We were sure God had said "full-time," and yet we experienced some very difficult times making ends meet.

After four years, we found ourselves following Bob's advice. My wife had a job at a Christian college which allowed weekends and the summer to travel, and I was writing and designing advertising for Christian organizations. We may have saved a lot of trouble by listening in the first place.

And finally, we can have direct access to the mind of God through His Spirit. But for years I struggled trying to hear. "Lord, I'm listening, but I don't hear anything."

For years I listened for this booming FM-radio-announcer voice with lots of echo effect. And of course

He would speak with "thous" and "shalts" and "verilys".

However, I finally made the shocking discovery that God sounds like Jim Watkins. Read Romans 12:2 again. As our minds are transformed, God speaks through our thoughts – He sounds like *you!*

But *how* can I know they're God's thoughts?!

2. How can I be sure it's God's Spirit?

Bob and Cindy's relationship has become more and more physical since they announced their engagement. Both have been raised in the church and know premarital sex is outside of God's will. But after they pray about it, the "Holy Spirit" assures them "intercourse is okay, since you are promised to one another."

The "Holy Spirit" tells the president of the local Women's Missionary Society "the white children of the neighborhood orphanage can be bused to Sunday school, but not the destructive black kids."

Rick and Sandy *know* the "Holy Spirit" has called them into full-time music ministry. They drop out of college, get married, and hock everything they own to buy sound equipment and a customized van.

Bob and Cindy broke up three months before the wedding. The orphanage director labeled the WMS president a bigot and refused to send any children to that Sunday school. Rick and Sandy sat across from me at McDonalds. Between sips of Coke, the couple bitterly accused God of leading them astray.

"We were so sure God was telling us to travel full-time with our music and look what happened – we're up to our ears in debt, we don't have any services scheduled, and Sandy's pregnant!"

How can we know what thoughts are truly God's? Each of these individuals were sincere Christians honestly wanting to know what God had planned for them. But unfortunately, when we pray, "God, speak to me" there is often a whirl of conflicting thoughts.

InterVarsity Christian Fellowship has an interesting way to tack down those thoughts so we can work with them. They suggest dividing a piece of paper down the middle. On one side write "advantages" and on the other "disadvantages." Or write "right/wrong", "good points/bad points" – whatever fits your issue or decision.

"God, I have presented myself to You, I am obeying You as closely as I know how, and I'm being careful in what I allow to come into my mind. God, use my 'transformed mind' to evaluate this issue or decision."

I've been amazed at the unique insights God has placed in my mind during these times. I have usually ended up with one column full and the other with just a few items. Rather than a blur of thoughts, they are neatly arranged so I can ask God for further insight into the issue.

If the list comes out even, look to see if some points outweigh others. Remember, too, that *any* direct command from Scripture will outbalance any number of items on the other side.

It has also been helpful to try to analyze which thoughts are coming from where. John Wesley warned, "Do not hastily ascribe things to God. Do not easily suppose dreams, voices, impressions, visions, or revelations to be from God. They may be from Him. They may be nature. They may be from the devil. Therefore, believe not every spirit, but 'try the spirits whether they be from God.' "

Even our "renewed minds" can receive input from four different sources:

1. Our own thoughts.

If you've taken a psychology class, you know just how incredibly complex the mind is. It can play games with us – without our even being aware of it.

I'm fairly sure Bob and Cindy were sincere in their prayer. But I'm also fairly certain they wanted the "answer" they received. They forgot that the Holy Spirit never tells us to do anything contrary to God's written Word, and so convinced themselves that premarital sex was OK.

Many times, people who declare "God told me to . . ." are only using it as a spiritual smoke screen around their own desires. I shudder at some of the things "the Holy Spirit convicts" some people to do!

2. Satan's thoughts

The popular idea that Satan flees when Christians pray didn't work for our Lord. Jesus spent 40 days in the wilderness praying and fasting. Yet it was at that time Satan tempted Him.

Satan comes as an "angel of light" – sounding very biblical. Remember, it was with out-of-context scripture that he tempted Christ. The closer we get to God, the harder Satan tries to wedge his thoughts into our minds.

3. Others' thoughts

Throughout Scripture God makes it very clear: We will become exactly like those we hang around with. If you want to be a winner, find some winners for friends. Want to be a loser, find some whiners for friends. If you want to excel spiritually, find those who are doing just that and make them your best friends.

"Birds of a feather do flock together!" (Just look around the cafeteria at school.) And *your* thinking will be shaped by those you choose to be with.

4. God's thoughts

The Holy Spirit *does* reveal His will through our thoughts. And Martin Wells Knapp shares four ways to make sure they are indeed God's thoughts:

(1) God's thoughts will *always* agree with Scripture.

The Women's Missionary Society president did have a verse from Genesis as her "proof text", but the Spirit will never ask us to do anything contrary to the *WHOLE* Bible. (Remember how we can justify almost anything with an out-of-context verse from Ecclesiastes?) But His thoughts will always be in keeping with the command to love Him with all our heart, soul, and mind, and our neighbor as ourselves.

(2) God's thoughts *always* agree with His righteousness.

John was convinced God wanted him in the military chaplaincy, but he was also convinced they wouldn't take him with his health problems. He struggled with his conscience. Should he lie on the application concerning his medical history? Or should he tell the truth and trust God for the outcome?

Knapp writes, "Impressions which are from God are always right. They may be contrary to our feelings, our prejudices, and our natural inclinations, but they are always right. They will stand the test."

(3) God's thoughts will *always* become reality.

Brian and Carl each knew for sure God was "calling" him into the pastorate. Brian had some problems getting the money together. But eventually circumstances worked out so he could attend college. Studies were also difficult, but with some tutoring, he graduated, and is now Minister of Youth at a large church.

Carl didn't pass his SAT test. His high school GPS was 1.9 and no college would even consider him. He's now working on a job where he has been able to lead several to Christ.

Cathy knew God wanted her in South America as a missionary. She had dreamed about it all her life. But she didn't pass the psychological testing. She tried another missions board, was accepted, but couldn't get a visa. She finally was hired by a third missions organization as a recruiter.

Many times our specific "visions" don't become a reality. Carl and Cathy misinterpreted their dreams. They're doing great things for God – just in a different setting than they planned.

But if God has genuinely spoken to you about a particular area, He will work out all the details.

(4) God's thoughts will *always* be reasonable.

The King James Version translates Romans 12:1 as *reasonable service*. God will never ask us to do something totally absurd.

"God has given us reasoning powers for a purpose," explains Knapp. "He respects them, appeals to them, and all of His leadings are in unison with them."

It is spiritually irresponsible to expect God to make all our decisions. Our own thoughts do play an important part in the process.

God does want to "speak" to us. He does want to give us direction and insight into various issues. But it is *rarely* a burning bush experience. It is seldom an audible voice.

It is more likely the combination of scriptural principles, our impressions, and the advice of other believers, all pointing in the same direction.

Oh, the depth of the riches of the wisdom and knowledge of God! How unsearchable his judgments, and his paths beyond tracing out! Who has known the mind of the Lord? . . . Therefore, I urge you, broth-

ers, in view of God's mercy, to offer your bodies as living sacrifices, holy and pleasing to God – which is your spiritual act of worship. Do not conform any longer to the pattern of this world, but be transformed by the renewing of your mind. Then you will be able to test and approve what God's will is – his good, pleasing and perfect will (Romans 11:33-34; 12:1-2).

For further reading . . .

> Psalm 119:97-99
> Proverbs 1:1-7; 2:1-12
> Proverbs 3:5-6
> John 14:25-27; 16:8-15
> Romans 8:5-8
> Romans 11:33–12:1
> 1 Corinthians 2:6-16

Affirming the Will of God by Paul Little (Intervarsity Press)

Emotions: Can You Trust Them? by James Dobson (Regal Books)

Lord, Change Me by Evelyn Christenson (Victor Books)

IV. What do others say about purple sweat socks?

1. The youth group and the church board

Pastor Jim, I've gone through those seven guidelines in 1 Corinthians 10 and I know the answer to the question a few weeks ago. You know, 'Should a Christian wear purple sweat socks?' " (I couldn't see what color socks were under her boots.) "Here's what I've found . . ."

"Wait, you can't do that, Jennifer."

"Come on!" the group protested. "Why not!?"

"Well, number one it will take away all the fun for the rest of us if Jennifer thinks for us. And like we've said, her answer may not be God's answer for the rest of us.

"We all need to think these issues through on our own. But most of all, God says in Romans 14:22 'Whatever you believe about these things keep between yourself and God.' "

"Why is that?!" (That came from Mike, of course.)

"Paul was talking about some red-hot issues in his day. Remember, these were questions that had no specific answer in the Bible, but each member had some very specific opinions. I think God gave Paul this command to avoid a big church split. So if someone asked his opinion, he probably pulled out a scrap of parchment with those seven questions penned on it."

For the rest of the meeting we discussed:

1. How do splits start?

The issue wasn't purple sweat socks, but Christ's disciples had their share of heated arguments: Who's in charge of refreshments for this cruise? Who's the most influential member? Wasn't that poor stewardship to let that lady pour all that expensive perfume on you? And I'm sure the annual church meeting at the First Church of Corinth included some interesting discussions!

But what is it that causes loving Christians to have such deep differences . . . and sometimes splits? Let's look at some biblical examples:

(1) A lack of understanding caused divisions.

Then John's disciples came and asked him, "How is it that we and the Pharisees fast, but your disciples do not fast? . . ." (Matthew 9:14).

Matthew 26:6-9 gives us another example of misunderstandings. *While Jesus was in Bethany . . . a woman came to him with an alabaster jar of very expensive perfume, which she poured on his head as he was reclining at the table.*

When the disciples saw this, they were indignant. "Why this waste?" they asked. "This perfume could have been sold at a high price and the money given to the poor."

If you've ever been club treasurer, Sunday school helper, head of the church nursery or youth president, you know how misunderstood leaders are. The issue may be as simple as your choice of crepe paper colors, but inevitably some dear saint will question your motives and intentions.

No matter how frustrated Christ became with His disciples, He always took time to pull them aside and explain His actions. Even that wasn't enough on this occasion. Right after the perfume affair Judas stormed out and offered to turn Christ over to the chief priests.

Unfortunately, no matter how well we explain, we will be misunderstood by a few fellow believers.

(2) Love of controversy caused divisions.

I was a lot like Mike during high school. I asked my share of divisive questions during youth fellowship and Sunday school. Talk-show hosts had trained me well in pitting one group against another group in discussions. It was loads of fun. But it was also destructive. The senior teen class went through five teachers during my three-year stay.

Sincere questioning of traditional thought is essential. But we need to be careful not to fall into the trap of creating controversy just for the sake of controversy.

One gutsy pastor I know "fired" two church board members for causing dissension in the church. (After all, in Galatians 5:20, God lumps it in the same category with idolatry and witchcraft.) The pastor's policy is this: "Rant and rave to your heart's content in board meetings. But after the vote, your responsibility as a board member is over. Everyone is to support the decision of the board to the rest of the church."

Paul goes even further. There are some things not worth ranting about. Don't have *an unhealthy interest in controversies and quarrels about words that result in envy, strife, malicious talk, evil suspicions and constant friction* (1 Timothy 6:4-5).

Don't have anything to do with foolish and stupid arguments, because you know they produce quarrels (2 Timothy 2:23).

(3) Unforgiveness caused divisions

There will always be those in our fellowship who

have made the wrong decisions or choices. As soon as rumors started that Sheila was pregnant, she was asked by the board not to attend the high school Sunday school class or teen choir. ("She will be a poor influence.") Sheila disappeared from my home church. The bitterness caused by such rejection caused her to give up her faith in the church and finally in God.

Admittedly, she did make a bad choice. But she needed the love and concern of the church, now more than ever. Christ states there is only one "unpardonable" sin. Unfortunately, we have made many issues "unpardonable" in the church.

God's forgiveness is greater than any sin or poor choice. We must forgive others, if we expect God to forgive us!

(4) Trying to fit others into our mold caused division.

In Romans 12:4-6 and 1 Corinthians 12:18-26 we find a wonderful paradox. We are one in Christ, and yet we are each very different. God has created us with unique talents and abilities, so in the diversity of the church we can have a wide-reaching work. "The First Church of the Clones" would have a very limited ministry!

But in fact God has arranged the parts [of the church] every one of them, just as he wanted them to be (1 Corinthians 12:18).

Where else but in the church can you find liberals, conservatives; Democrats, Republicans; extroverts, introverts; white collar, blue collar; young, old; short, tall; fat and thin; all loving one another and working together? At least that is God's intention.

(5) Pride and prejudice caused divisions.

My views on a particular issue are mine. They have been worked out between my two ears, in my brain, and are a personal part of me. When someone challenges those findings, I often take it personally. "They are attacking *me.*" And before I know it, my pride is hurt, and division is underway.

One of the most valuable lessons I learned in Journalism 101 was to develop "tough skin." With terror and humiliation I would open letters from publishers. Weeks earlier I had sent them my best article filled with well-written anecdotes, great character development, and a strong theme that leaped out from every page. This was the masterpiece I had spent sleepless nights developing in my mind.

And now some heartless editor, who obviously doesn't know good writing when he sees it, has attached a form letter to my creation, claiming "it does not fit our editorial needs at this time."

Finally, I'm realizing that the rejection of my ideas is not a rejection of me as a person. I am not that manuscript. I am not even the color of paint for the men's restroom! I am loved by the God of the universe. My value comes from knowing He has created me. Don't allow pride to cause division at home or church.

Another major problem facing the early church was what to do with the Gentile believers. The coming of the Holy Spirit didn't immediately sweep away Jewish pride and prejudice. Remember the Apostle Peter had to have his famous "integration vision" after Pentecost (Acts 10).

It must have been difficult for Peter, who had been taught all his life, "Don't take candy from strangers and never talk to Gentiles," to hear there was no race distinction in Christ. (God had to show him this spectacular vision three times to convince him!)

Likewise, it is difficult for us to accept others who feel the opposite we do on issues. But if there is no biblical condemnation of the particular action, we must accept and encourage that person regardless of their views and opinions. As in Peter's case, this isn't always easy, but God wants to help us.

But what do we do if the whole church is divided over purple sweat socks? (The "pro-purples" now sit on the left side of the church and the "Citizens Against

Purple Sweat Socks'' sit on the right.) The book of Acts gives us a model for confronting in the church:

2. How to stop splits

Some men came down from Judea to Antioch and were teaching the brothers: "Unless you are circumcised, according to the custom taught by Moses, you cannot be saved." This brought Paul and Barnabas into sharp dispute and debate with them (Acts 15:1-2).

Here's how they handled the controversy:

(1) They met to discuss it face-to-face (v. 3)

Rather than telling their friends how awful it was what those guys from Judea were doing, they personally confronted them. Christ demands in Matthew 18:15 that we go to that person and *show him his fault, just between the two of you.*

Paul puts it this way, *Brothers, if someone is caught in a sin, you who are spiritual should restore him gently. But watch yourself, or you also may be tempted. Carry each other's burdens, and in this way you will fulfill the law of Christ* (Galatians 6:1-2).

James agrees, *My brothers, if one of you should wander from the truth and someone should bring him back, remember this: Whoever turns a sinner from the error of his way will save him from death and cover over a multitude of sins* (James 5:19-20).

But many have used out-of-context verses to avoid confronting. "We can't judge anyone!" That's true, but look at our legal system. You'll notice the juries only try to discern innocence or guilt. For every verse that says "don't judge," there is another that says we will know what is inside of people by their actions, their words, and the "fruit" they are producing.

We are definitely not to go around passing sentence on the guilty (that is the judge's and God's job). But when we sense that a Christian friend is violating clear scriptural principles, it is our responsibility to lovingly confront them.

My Executive Editor friend asked me into his office one day and closed the door. ("Hmmmm, I think I'm in trouble.)

"Jim, you're doing a great job with the magazine and I'm getting a lot of good letters about the improvements." (Now, I know I'm in trouble. He's softening me up for the kill.)

"I don't want to talk to you as a fellow editor, I want to talk to you as a friend." (Well, at least my agency hasn't lost the contract.)

"I'm just concerned that your humor is sometimes very bitter, and I'm afraid it will someday hinder your writing and speaking ministry. There seems to be a lot of anger and resentment smoldering inside of you."

That was too much honesty! I started crying. (I hadn't done that since *Chariots of Fire*.)

"You bet I'm angry. I'm furious that my son and daughter have to grow up in a world that is being perverted and debased by Satan. Every time I watch the news I see God's creations being butchered, and bombed, and mugged and raped. I am so mad at Satan I can't stand it."

For the next two hours we talked about the world situation, and we talked about ways in which God was working. By the time we were done we were both crying and hugging.

"Jim, that was one of the hardest things I've ever done. I'm just so glad we could talk about it and understand each other."

I was impressed that here was a man who cared enough to risk appearing nosy or interfering to help me. He was willing to pull away the protective layers I had built up to insulate myself.

(2) They lovingly appealed to personal testimony and Scripture (Acts 15:4, 7-18).

Paul and Barnabas share what the two factions have in common and how God has wonderfully worked through both. We need to approach those who disagree by using the same bridge-building techniques.

"I appreciate our friendship and the great way God is working through it. . . ."

James jumps in at this point and shows scriptural principles to back up their concern. It's interesting that the two with the "sharp dispute" work at rebuilding the relationship, and a third then shows the group their error.

Many times if we would spend more time caring, the other person would realize or confess the problem on their own. (Probably they know they're not pleasing God, but when attacked or cruelly confronted they'll become defensive and deny it.) Love breaks down barriers.

David Augsburger talks about this "care-fronting" in his book, *Caring Enough To Confront.*

> *I differ with you*
> > *(To differ is not to reject)*
> *I disagree with you*
> > *(To disagree is not to attack)*
> *I will confront you*
> > *(To confront is to compliment)*
> *I will invite change*
> > *(To change is to grow)*

(3) They came out of meeting with one voice in writing.

The people read it and were glad for its encouraging message (Acts 15:31).

I like the idea of putting it in writing for all to read in the bulletin or mid-week mailing. The Jerusalem Convention even sent out teams to answer questions on the decision.

The board I currently serve on is delightfully free of the tension I've felt on other committees. One reason is its *written* policy for just about everything: Who gets flowers for what illnesses and tragedies? Who can use the church buses? Who pays for the gas on youth outings? Who can borrow AV equipment? Who can use the church facilities? How much will it cost? Who schedules the pastor's counseling? Who can make decisions for what area of church ministry?

With a written policy there is no favoritism or inconsistency in the church operation. And it saves many hurt feelings!

(4) A spirit of unity came out of the "board meeting".

In Philippians, Paul encourages the church to be unified in its diversity. *All of us who are mature should take such a view of things. And if on some point you think differently, that too God will make clear to you* (Philippians 3:15).

Does this mean everyone should have the same answer to the purple-sweat-sock controversy? Should all votes in board meetings be unanimous? Read the context of the verse.

Paul says, I have not arrived spiritually *but I press on to take hold of that for which Christ Jesus took hold of me. Brothers, I do not consider myself yet to have taken hold of it. But one thing I do: Forgetting what is behind and straining toward what is ahead, I press on toward the goal to win the prize for which God has called me heavenward in Christ Jesus* (Philippians 3:12b-14).

We are to be united in the belief that . . .

We have not arrived spiritually, nor will we ever have enough maturity to know the final answer on every issue.

We shouldn't be looking back at our own mistakes or the mistakes of others.

We should all be looking at Christ and the final goal line, rather than comparing ourselves with others in the race.

The color of our running outfits (don't forget socks), our bone and muscle structure, and our running style are all different in this race. Having the same

Coach and common goal unites us!

Does your group need a fund-raising project? Instead of washing cars make plaques to sell. Use this proverb, and make sure every church member buys one:

> IN ESSENTIALS, UNITY
> IN NON-ESSENTIALS, LIBERTY
> IN ALL THINGS, CHARITY

For further reading . . .

Matthew 7:1-5, 15-20
John 17:20-23
Acts 2:42-47
Romans 14:1–15:7
1 Corinthians 12:12-31
Ephesians 4:1-6
2 Timothy 2:25-26
James 4:11-12

2. Friends and parents

T here I am wearing bell-bottom jeans, a flowered shirt, and peach-fuzz sideburns. I still cringe when I look at those pictures from the late sixties. And I'm sure my parents must have cringed at the time, but they were either very open-minded or very close-mouthed when it came to number-one son's choice of school clothes!

But what should we do when Mom and Dad declare, "You will (or will not) wear purple sweat socks?" What should we do when our friends disagree with our position on an issue? The question is easier when both parents and friends are biblical Christians. We know they have our best interest – physically, mentally, socially, and spiritually – at heart. Discussion is easier because all have the same basic values and beliefs.

But if you have unbelieving parents, Christ warns it is going to be tough.

"Do you think I came to bring peace on earth? No, I tell you, but division. From now on there will

be five in one family divided against each other, three against two and two against three. They will be divided, father against son and son against father, mother against daughter and daughter against mother, mother-in-law against daughter-in-law and daughter-in-law against mother-in-law" (Luke 12:51-53).

Paul also states that Christian and non-Christian relationships are strained at best. *For what do righteousness and wickedness have in common? Or what fellowship can light have with darkness? What harmony is there between Christ and Belial? What does a believer have in common with an unbeliever?* (2 Corinthians 6:14b-15).

I've talked with teens whose parents have punished them by denying church attendance. And unbelieving parents have refused to help with college expenses because their teen chose a Christian school rather than their alma mater.

Some of the divisions and conflicts have been self-imposed, though. Stan was constantly preaching "hell, fire, and brimstone" to his "heathen mother." He would sneak out, when "grounded," to come to youth meeting and was always asking prayer for "that sinful woman."

When I visited the home, I did meet a slightly drunk, but also a very confused mother. "He comes home ranting and raving how awful I am. Stan's a good boy and I don't want him in some crazy cult. You're not a crazy cult leader, are you?"

I tried to assure her I wasn't. But I've tried to ask myself how I would react if my son became involved in a "strange" religion. For instance, there was Bob – the strangest kid in the junior high! One week he would claim to be an extraterrestrial and the next the reincarnation of Attila the Hun. He even brought his "god" to school in a box – "Kozgro McOrlo Excellsior."

How would I feel if my son came home from school as a devout follower of "Kozgro"?

"I've tried to teach Paul right, but all he wants to do is go over to Bob's house and worship this god in a box. He has been more loving and polite since his 'conversion.' Sometimes I wonder if it might even help me. But his new beliefs make me feel uncomfortable and I feel hurt that he seems to love this 'Kozgro' thing more than his family. He gives me the impression it's more important to obey this god than me, his father.''

Try to see your actions and attitudes from Mom and Dad's point of view; or from the eyes of the play director at school who doesn't understand why you can't skip youth meeting for a few weeks; or the manager at McDonald's who's frustrated because you won't work on Sundays.

But Christians have been misunderstood from the beginning. First-century unbelievers asked, ''Are these Christians cannibals? They talk about getting together to 'drink Christ's blood and eat His body.' ''

''I'm not letting my daughter go to one of those 'love feasts' where they engage in 'holy kisses'!''

''That's nothing. I overheard one of them talking about expecting some sort of extraterrestrial king to beam down and overthrow the government!''

Now, most of us have grown up with communion, carry-in dinners, and sermons about the return of Christ. But these concepts were absolutely foreign to unbelievers in A.D. 40.

Likewise, the whole idea of a superior being is absurd to a humanist. He believes that all there is to reality is impersonal matter and energy thrown together and evolved by chance into its present form. Carl Sagan, on PBS's ''Cosmos'' declared, ''The cosmos is all that is or ever was or ever will be.''

That view makes sense to a man living in a two-dimensional world — only matter and energy. All he knows is length and width. How can a two-dimensional person possibly understand depth? That is why it is impossible for the dwellers of ''Flatland'' to comprehend the three-dimensional Christian (matter, energy, and spirit)!

Other concepts don't make sense in a two-dimensional land: Christ's blessings on the ''poor in spirit, the meek, the merciful, the pure in heart," don't compute in a looking-out-for-number-one world. And "love your enemy" makes even less sense to that world.

So many of our friends and family members may have a difficult time understanding our love for the true God — just as I would have a difficult time understanding my son becoming a follower of "Kozgro McOrlo Excellsior." We can expect division. But don't intentionally add to it!

1. Don't make a big deal out of saying grace at home or in the school cafeteria.

Never use your hometown-team-touchdown voice to proclaim, "Lord, I thank Thee that I am not one of these godless heathens who gulp down their soyburgers without giving their Creator due thanks!"

2. Don't embarrass your friends or parents by wearing outrageous religious buttons (e.g. "Live to beat hell!") or carrying a fifteen-pound Bible everywhere you go.

3. Don't disobey Mom and Dad in the name of the church.

God doesn't say, "Honor your father and mother (only if they are both Christians) so that you may live long in the land." You'll only add to their belief that "religion has made you rebellious."

But what if they ask you to do something the Bible says is wrong? We'll talk about that in the next chapter.

4. Don't neglect your household chores to read your fifteen-pound Bible.

If you think being grounded for reading the Bible is almost as saintly as being burned at the stake, think again.

5. Don't sit around the house looking like a clock with the hands stuck at twenty past eight if they punish you by forbidding church activities for a week.

You can see your Christian friends at school and probably have more time for your personal devotions. A week without church activities won't hurt you in the long run.

6. Don't use "church-ese."

You might as well speak New Testament Greek, as to use terms unbelievers don't understand. Avoid terms like Beulah Land, blessing, born again, burdened, burdens are lifted, carnal, conviction, deep sin (as opposed to shallow!), door of your heart, fleece, grace, hell fire, Holy Ghost, The Lamb, nailed to the cross, opened door, over Jordan, rapture, redeemed, repent, revival, sanctified, saved, sin, soul-winner, total commitment, Trinity, turn or burn, washed in the blood, the Word.

You too will understand God and His purpose better if you are forced to put church-ese terms into simple English. For example, sin is disobedience or indifference toward God. To a "sinner," sin means something really gross: multiple murders or armed robbery. So they've probably never done anything that they would consider sinful.

7. Don't force your faith on your friends or parents.

Intimidation may work for the Mafia and collection agencies, but it will turn those you love against your beliefs.

8. Don't attack their beliefs, but be able to calmly and reasonably share your beliefs.

Paul and Peter give us this advice in Colossians 4 and 1 Peter 3.

Be wise in the way you act toward outsiders; make the most of every opportunity. Let your conversation be always full of grace, seasoned with salt, so that you may know how to answer everyone Colossians 4:5-6, author's bold type).

As I've shared from the beginning of this book, "Well . . . ah . . . my church believes" is not an adequate answer for why we believe as we do.

Always be prepared to give an answer to everyone who asks you to give the reason for the hope that you have. But do this with gentleness and respect, keeping a clear conscience, so that those who speak maliciously against your good behavior in Christ may be ashamed of their slander (1 Peter 3:15b-16, author's bold type).

Many unbelievers will try to dodge the real issues by trying to appear "spiritual." They try to soothe their consciences (and ours) with statements such as these:

"It's not so important what you believe, as long as you believe something."

"Jesus was a very good man, but I don't believe He was really God."

But Christianity is not based on beliefs or even on faith. If faith was the issue, Bob would have found real love, peace and joy through "Kosgro McOrlo Excellsior." But no matter how much faith Bob has in this "god in a box" it won't meet the real needs of his life. A strong and sincere faith does absolutely nothing for us if what we believe in is not reliable.

So faith doesn't save us – but it is faith *in Christ* that brings eternal life. Josh McDowell, Francis Schaeffer and C. S. Lewis have shown us that the Christian faith is a reasonable faith. (We don't have to check our brains at the church door!)

(1) Christianity is based on historical fact.

In *Evidence That Demands a Verdict*, Josh McDowell stresses that Christianity is not "blind faith," but rather "intelligent faith." The Apostle Paul said, "I know whom I have believed" and urges us to "prove all things." Jesus said, *You will know the truth and the truth will set you free* (John 8:32).

Paul Little in *Know Why You Believe* states that "Faith in Christianity is based on evidence. It is reasonable faith. Faith in the Christian sense goes beyond reason, but not against it."

And in *Whatever Happened to the Human Race?* Schaeffer makes a strong case for Christianity based on the reliability of its history.

"Christianity involves history. To say only that, is already to have said something remarkable, because it separates the Judeo-Christian worldview from almost all other religious thought. It is rooted in history.

"Is the history accurate? The more we understand about the Middle East between 2,500 B.C. and A.D. 100, the more confident we can be that the information in the Bible is reliable, even when it speaks about the simple things of time and space.

"If Jesus did not live, or if He did not rise from the dead, Christianity cannot continue. It cannot live on a mere idea, because Christianity is about objective truth and not merely religious experiences. Both the Old Testament and the New Testament claim to be truth . . . truth rooted in history."

(2) Christianity is based on a historical Jesus.

No unbiased historian can ever doubt Christ's presence in history. At least nine *secular* historians, between A.D. 80 and 150, wrote of Christ as an *actual* person.

But if Christ cannot be explained away historically, unbelievers will try to strip Him of His deity. "Yes," they admit, "He was a very good man, but He was not God." C. S. Lewis challenges that logic. He claims that Christ could not possibly have been just a good man. He was either Lord, a liar, or a lunatic.

A psychiatrist walked into a mental ward and

asked the first patient his name. "I'm Napoleon!" the man confidently responded."

"Oh, and who told you that you are Napoleon?"

"God told me," was the reply.

"I didn't say such a thing!" shouted the man in the second bed.

People who claim to be God are usually kept confined, and not usually labeled as "good men."

But in John 10:30 Jesus claims, *"I and the Father are one."* He announces that He is eternal: *"Before Abraham was born, I am"* (John 8:58). In John 14:9 Jesus proclaims, *"Anyone who has seen me has seen the Father."* And throughout His ministry, Christ claimed to be able to forgive sins (Mark 2:5, Luke 7:48): something reserved for God alone.

So let's look at Christ's claim to be God, and look at the alternatives as C. S. Lewis lists them.

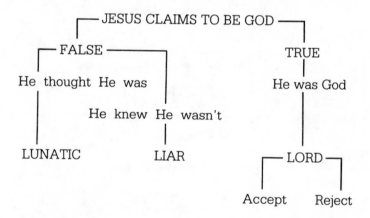

(3) Christianity works in history.

The most convincing "proofs" of the reality of Christ will be our changed lives. Unbelievers need to "see" Christ living through you and me — at school, at work, and particularly at home.

We *can* be sure of the "reason for our hope." If you're not, run, don't walk, to the nearest library or

Christian bookstore for one of the books listed at the end of this chapter.

For further reading . . .

Romans 1:18-32

Escape From Reason by Francis Schaeffer (InterVarsity Press)
Evidence That Demands a Verdict by Josh McDowell (Campus Crusade For Christ)
True Spirituality by Francis Schaeffer (Tyndale House)
Whatever Happened to the Human Race? by Francis Schaeffer and C. Everett Koop (Fleming H. Revell)

3. Student Council, the Supreme Court

T he moment our pink little heads emerge into the bright lights of the outside world, we are under authority. The state board of health and the hospital administration have authorized this huge man in white to swat us on the behind. And Mom and Dad have legal custody of us until we're 18.

Add to that teachers, school and college administrators, Student Council, Selective Service, professional accrediting associations, pastors, church boards, union stewards, bosses, the I.R.S., loan committees, ad infinitum. We can't even die without the government's intervention with health restrictions and burial ordinances.

But what if the government (be it the high school principal or the Supreme Court) asks us to do something that violates our beliefs? Paul and Peter give us God's answer.

Everyone must submit himself to the governing authorities, for there is no authority except that which God has established. The authorities that exist have been established by God. Consequently, he who rebels against the authority is rebelling against what God has instituted, and those who do so will bring judgment on themselves. For rulers hold no terror **for those who do right,** *but for those who do wrong. Do you want to be free from fear of the one in authority? Then* **do what is right** *and he will commend you. For he is* **God's servant to do you good** (Romans 13:1-4a, author's bold type).

Submit yourselves for the Lord's sake to every authority instituted among men: whether to the king, as the supreme authority, or to governors, who are sent by him to punish those who do wrong and to **commend those who do right.** *For* **it is God's will that by doing good** *you should silence the ignorant talk of foolish men. Live as free men, but do not use your freedom as a cover-up for evil;* **live as servants of God** (1 Peter 2:13-16, author's bold type).

Notice the bold type. We are only required to obey an authority which is promoting what is right and good in God's eyes. This same Peter along with John had to decide whether to obey man or God on one such occasion.

Then Peter, filled with the Holy Spirit, said to them: "Rulers and elders of the people! If we are being called to account today for an act of kindness shown to a cripple and are asked how he was healed, then know this, you and all the people of Israel: It is by the name of Jesus Christ. . . ."

[The rulers] commanded them not to speak or teach at all in the name of Jesus. But Peter and John replied, "Judge for yourselves whether it is right in God's sight to obey you rather than God. For we cannot help speaking about what we have seen and heard" (Acts 4:8-10a, 18-20).

Samuel Rutherford declared that God's Law is King. And if the king (small k) disobeys the Law (capital L), then the king is to be disobeyed. His A.D. 1600 book suggests four steps to follow when an authority asks us to violate *clear biblical* principles.

1. Protest legally within the system.

In a democratic country we have the privilege to voice our opposition through hundreds of legal avenues – suggestion boxes, petitions, rallies, marches, organized boycotts, letters to the editor, paid advertisements, picketing, and sit-ins. Many organizations have been set up to lobby for legislation that would assure government that reflects God's sovereign principles. The same groups also provide voting records of representatives, so that we can vote for those who agree with us on the issue.

But before you write a letter to the editor or organize a school "walkout," make sure you:

(1) Know the enemy – Make sure it's God's enemy.

Unfortunately, church members are often so busy fighting each other, they don't have time to fight the enemy. Many spend their time running around blowing out matches (minor and trivial issues) when a forest fire is raging outside the door.

I have a friend who is constantly reminding me to "choose your battles." We can't fight every evil in our world, but we can concentrate on the most significant ones. Tackle the big issues and–

(2) Don't get caught up in a one-issue campaign unless God specifically directs you.

Fight the *root causes* rather than the resulting symptoms or issues. Many church historians claim that while the church was preaching against the evils of liquor, before the days of prohibition, humanism was creeping in unnoticed and unchallenged.

In the past some preachers spent entire sermons on such topics as "the evil of ladies' seamless hose." I'm not sure what the text was, but the idea was this: If the stockings had a seam up the back, you at least knew if her legs were properly covered. (And you thought the purple sweat sock "controversy" was far-fetched!)

(3) Be informed, be credible.

Civil rights leader, Martin Luther King, Jr., warned that two vital phases of a nonviolent campaign were "the collection of facts to determine whether injustices exist, and self-purification." Not only must our hearts be right, but our facts straight.

For the past several years, well-meaning pastors and congregations have been burying the Federal Communications Commission with petitions. They want to protest "an attempt by Madeline Murray O'Hare to ban all religious broadcasting from the air-waves." Millions of Christians have responded to this letter-writing appeal. In truth, no such action is even being considered by the F.C.C.

During my junior year, a local pastor went to the school board to condemn the reading of *Catcher in the "Raw."* Not only did he become the laughingstock of the community for not knowing the correct title, but he had to admit he had never read (or even seen) the book.

Attacking the issue before we have the facts doesn't fit Peter and Paul's strategies in the last chapter.

(4) Do as much praying as you do plotting.

The combination of prayer and legal protest is powerful!

For though we live in the world, we do not wage war as the world does. The weapons we fight with are not the weapons of the world. On the contrary, they have divine power to demolish strongholds. We demolish arguments and every pretension that sets itself up against the knowledge of God, and we take captive every thought to make it obedient to Christ (2 Corinthians 10:3-5).

If my people, who are called by my name, will

humble themselves and pray and seek my face and turn from their wicked ways, then will I hear from heaven and will forgive their sin and heal their land (2 Chronicles 7:14).

(5) Provide a positive alternative to the actions you are protesting.

Abby Hoffman, one of the radical leaders of the late sixties wrote *Revolution for the Hell of It*. Anarchy and disorganization were better than bad government according to the author. But we should never become involved in an issue merely to condemn the issue. We need to provide a Christian alternative for the things we want to eliminate.

John Wesley not only preached against the heartless treatment of the working class during the industrial revolution, but provided practical alternatives to the abuses he saw. The Methodists set up free clinics, opened the first employees credit union, and built orphanages. Even secular historians admit that the work of John Wesley and his followers saved England from a British version of the French Revolution. His involvement changed the government!

(6) Be prepared for criticism and welcome it.

Critics can help us clarify and seriously think through our own beliefs. Plato claimed they were "the unpaid guardians of my soul."

Francis Schaeffer, Surgeon General C. Everett Koop, and groups such as The Moral Majority, have been criticized for their strong stands on issues. No matter what your view, they should have all our respect for caring enough to confront. No change will come from discussions in Sunday school or sermons in church. There must be action!

But make sure you have exhausted every legal avenue before going on to stronger confrontations.

2. Flee if at all possible.

My parents had very strong views against dancing. So when our junior high gym class had dance
classes for three weeks, I was allowed to write a report
in the library on basketball. Most teachers are willing
to provide alternative assignments if there is an objec-
tion to a particular book or subject.

You may choose to change schools, join a different
church, or move out of town. In a more complex society than A.D. 1600, however, "fleeing" may not be
possible. Rutherford then suggests that after trying
every possible legal action–

3. Rebel

And God's people have been a rebellious lot! John
Brashaw claims that "Rebellion against tyrants is
obedience to God." Moses demanded, "Let my people
go!" Gideon and Samson were both guilty of destroying public property. Daniel was the first to run into
the problem of a government's laws against prayer.
Shadrach, Meshach, and Abednego refused the king's
orders to bow to the golden idol.

Christ defied the Pharisees' rules and regulations,
and throughout early church history Christians resisted
Roman rule.

William Tyndale (1490-1536), the famous Bible
translator, evaded the authorities for years. He was finally executed for stressing the supremacy of Scripture
over human law.

John Knox (1515-1572) began teaching reformation
ideas during the time of Luther, and is credited with
justifying revolution against governments that ruled
contrary to the Bible.

John Bunyan (1628-1688) was arrested three times
for preaching without a state license and not attending
the Church of England. Bunyon wrote *Pilgrim's Pro-
gress* while in jail.

Martin Luther King, Jr. (1929-1968) and his followers also spent a lot of time in jail. He warned,

"One who breaks an unjust law must do so openly, lovingly, and with a willingness to accept the penalty. I submit that an individual who breaks a law that conscience tells him is unjust, and who willingly accepts the penalty of imprisonment in order to arouse the conscience of the community over its injustice, is in reality expressing the highest respect for law."

4. Use force if necessary.

Francis Schaeffer claims that force is sometimes necessary. "I am not a pacifist. Pacifism in this lost world means that we desert the people who need our greatest help.

"Suppose I am walking down the street and see a burly man beating a little girl to death. I plead with him to stop. If we don't, what does love mean? Love means I stop him any way I can, including hitting him.

"If I desert the little girl to the bully, I have deserted the true meaning of Christian love and responsibility to my neighbor" *(Moody Monthly,* October 1982).

Dietrich Bonhoeffer (1906-1945) was a German theologian who worked to overthrow the Nazi regime. Bonhoeffer was eventually hanged for his part in a widespread conspiracy to assassinate Adolf Hitler. This minister concluded, "It is not only my task to look after the victims of madmen who drive a motorcar in a crowded street, but to do all in my power to stop their driving at all."

When we take a bold stand, based on strong scriptural principles, persecution is always a possibility. But there is something even worse—

The early Christians had taken their stand for Christ against the Roman State. The rulers couldn't have cared less what anyone believed about religion. But it would not put up with what they viewed as anti-government beliefs. Thus the inhumane persecution mentioned earlier.

But when Constantine became a Christian in A.D. 313, persecution abruptly stopped. By 318 the ruler had declared Christianity the state religion. But making Christianity the socially accepted norm is a worse disaster than persecution. Following Christ must always mean a harder, narrower path, or the church becomes watered down by the uncommitted.

Sure enough, as a political organization, the church steadily declined in morals and holiness until the reformation in the 1500s! Christianity cannot survive popularity. It cannot survive when wrapped in the flag of any nation. We need to work for laws that reflect God's principles, but avoid the kind of "theocracy" that almost destroyed the faith for more than a thousand years.

No matter what the issues or the form of confrontation, we need to use wisdom and make sure that God has *specifically* instructed us to *specific* action on a *specific* scripturally based issue.

For further reading . . .

Judges 6:13-32
Daniel 3, 6
Matthew 17:24-27
Acts 4:1-22, 5:17-42
Romans 13:1-7

A Christian Manifesto by Francis Schaeffer (Crossway Books)
The Second American Revolution by John W. Whitehead (David C. Cook)

V. What do you think about purple sweat socks?

I should let you know that Mike now feels purple sweat socks aren't for him. Jennifer concluded that they were fine for her. They've also decided that dating each other is also very fine.

I trust you now have the tools to work through your issue of purple sweat socks or ——. Feel free to photocopy additional copies of the following charts for your personal use in deciding if other issues are right or wrong for you.

And do remember that *knowing* what's right and wrong is only a part of God's plan for your life—

Who is wise and understanding among you? Let him show it by his good life, by deeds done in the humility that comes from wisdom. But if you harbor bitter envy and selfish ambition in your hearts, do not boast about it or deny the truth. Such "wisdom" does not come down from heaven but is earthly, unspiritual, of the devil. For where you have envy and selfish ambition, there you find disorder and every evil practice.

But the wisdom that comes from heaven is first of all pure; then peace-loving, considerate, submissive, full of mercy and good fruit, impartial and sincere. Peacemakers who sow in peace raise a harvest of righteousness (James 3:13-18).

God bless you as you use these methods to decide "Should a Christian ——?"

Issue:

Specific scriptures that relate to this issue:

General scriptures that relate to this issue:
     ( ) It is beneficial and constructive.
     ( ) It is not mastering me
     ( ) It is motivated by God's love for others
     ( ) It produces a clear conscience
     ( ) It will not cause a weaker Christian to sin
     ( ) It is a glory to God
     ( ) It is good for my witness

Thoughts I sense God gave me concerning this issue:

Actions I need to take as a result of my position on this issue:

Leader's Guide

Dear Youth Leader,

I trust that you now know if purple sweat socks (or whatever) are right or wrong for you — but don't tell your teens! *Should a Christian wear purple sweat socks?* is designed to allow young people to discern what's right or wrong for them.

The thirteen-chapter format will allow you to use this book in an elective Sunday school class, a discipleship group or weekly youth meeting. (It will also come in handy when Mike asks you, "Should a Christian go to the prom? . . . drink socially? . . . become a surrogate father? . . . or whatever?" Just hand him the book and say, "Read this!")

Each session includes three sections:

1. Engage Interest is designed to shift the teens' thoughts from the day at school (or the good-looking visitor) to the topic.

2. Explore the Bible and Life will reinforce the

chapter just read, with Bible study and discussion. (Unless you have an exceptional group, many will NOT have read the assigned chapter. You may need to spend time reviewing the key points of the chapter before discussion is possible.)

3. Enact the Truth in Life stresses the practical ways to live out the session. This is the "homework"!

But most importantly, avoid discussion of specific issues. Keep reminding teens to plug in their question whenever they hear the phrase "purple sweat socks." This way they will discover what they believe and WHY. And that will hold up better under peer pressure at home or school than, "Pastor Jim says ——" or "My church believes ——."

Week 1: Who says purple sweat socks are right or wrong?

1. Engage Interest

☐ Option 1

Have teens sit in a circle. All extra chairs must be removed. Read each of the following statements. The teens move one chair to the right on the statements that apply to them. They should remain in their seats if the statement does not apply to them.

The result should be fun. With different people moving on different statements, there will be times when two or more teens will be occupying the same seat!

1. I think (name of current number-one Christian singer) is the best Christian singer. If you agree, move to the right. If you disagree stay seated.

2. A Christian should never, ever pull a dog's ear.

3. John is my favorite book in the New Testament.

4. My parents actually enjoy listening to (current heavy metal Christian group).

5. This is a ridiculous game.

6. A Christian should always agree with the pastor's sermon.

7. I have never worn a pair of purple sweat socks.

8. I am not sitting on anyone's lap right now.

9. Eating an entire bag of Oreos during one commercial is a sin.

10. There is nothing I would rather do than study *Should a Christian wear purple sweat socks?*

☐ Option 2

Have four "hams" in your youth group present the following skit of "Night Light" with Ted Toppel, Earnest Sincerely, "Tube" Turner, and the United States Surgeon General.

Toppel: Good evening, and welcome to "Night Light." I'm Ted Toppel, and with me in the studio is TV evangelist Earnest Sincerely, network executive "Tube" Turner, and the United States Surgeon General.

As you know, purple sweat socks have become a national obsession. Closed factories have retooled and are now producing the purple profit makers. And exports of the colorful footwarmers have effectively reduced the trade deficit and brought unemployment under one percent.

But purple sweat socks are not without their critics. Mr. Sincerely has launched a national campaign called "Wolves in Sheep's Stockings".

Sincerely: (with much fervor) Yes, my friends, just as demonic power entered the pigs in our Lord's time, the enemy has entered the sheep of this nation to produce this powerful plague of purple! Yes, the enemy has a foothold on the feet of our children, young people, and entire families with this idolatrous obsession! Our nation is knee-high in perversion. Soon America's moral fabric will be full of the holes of purple sweat socks! So repent, and turn from your purple ways before your foot slips into utter darkness!

Turner: (very smooth) Now just a moment, Mr. Sincerely. While I respect your personal beliefs concerning purple sweat socks, it is important to point out that this is an area of individual choice. As a network executive, my responsibility is to provide viewers with what they want to watch. And our Neilson ratings and huge demand for advertising time from purple sweat sock manufacturers would indicate that the public wants to see more purple sweat socks on television.

Toppel: Would the Surgeon General like to respond?

Surgeon: Yes I would. While not conclusive, our research is indicating that prolonged contact with purple sweat socks may be hazardous to your laboratory animal's health. It would seem the media and manufacturers have been reckless in their promotion of the purple sweat sock fad, even though it has known of the dangers for some time.

Sincerely: (Standing up) Gaaaaaalory! The Lord will punish those peddlers of purple perversion with a powerful purging plague!

Turner: Mr. Sincerely, need I remind you that my cable network carries your TV program. And may I also remind you that the contract is up for renewal in six weeks.

Sincerely: (Sitting down) Oh.

Toppel: Well, I think it's time for a commercial from one of our fine sponsors, "Sock It To You Industries," makers of (sheepishly) purple sweat socks.

Transition:
There is a wide variety of opinions on a wide variety of issues in our world. For the next few

weeks, we're going to discover how to decide what's right or wrong for each of us. Do you have an issue or question in mind? We'll discuss the hypothetical issue of purple sweat socks. Each time you hear the phrase "purple sweat socks", plug in the issue you're thinking about.

2. Explore the Bible and Life

Break into three groups. Have each group discuss one of the following Scripture portions:

Group 1: Romans 14:1-8

Group 2: Romans 14:9-18

Group 3: Romans 14:19-23

Have each group discover the main point of the verses. Group 1 should find that differences in the church are normal. Group 2 should observe that Christians shouldn't judge those who have different opinions. Group 3 should discover that differences shouldn't divide.

Then ask the entire group these questions:

1. What people or organizations are trying to tell us what's right and wrong?

2. Are spoon-fed values and beliefs really our own?

3. Why doesn't "my church believes" hold up under pressure?

4. According to the Scripture, will all Christians come to the same conclusion on "purple sweat socks"? Why? Why not?

5. How can I tell what's right or wrong?

3. Enact the Truth in Life

☐ Have teens write on one of the charts in the back of the book the issue(s) they are thinking about. Close in prayer for wisdom as the teens explore what's right and wrong for them.

Week 2: Specific principles from God's Word

1. Engage Interest
☐ Option 1

Before class, mount two pieces of construction paper on opposite ends of the meeting room. On one draw a huge **A** and on the other, a large **B**.

Tell your teens, **We're conducting an opinion poll. Run and stand under the "letter" of your answer to these multiple-choice questions:**

1. **When I play a video game for the first time, I (a) always read the instructions before inserting the token, or (b) pop in the token and play it as it comes.**
2. **When it comes to teachers, I like (a) hard but interesting ones, or (b) the boring, but easy graders.**
3. **When I buy something new I always (a) read the instructions completely before putting it together or turning it on, or (b) plug it in and see what happens.**
4. **When it comes to the Bible's instructions, I (a) follow it like I follow human instructions, or (b) follow it differently from human directions.**

☐ Option 2

Ask teens to react to the following situations with either (a) their head in their lap while holding on to their ankles (crash position for danger), (b) chewing fingernails for "slightly nervous," or (c) sitting normally for "no problem!"

1. **Welcome aboard Lameduck Airlines. This is your pilot speaking. We'll be flying at . . . oh, I'm not sure, whatever speed feels right, and an altitude of . . . well, we'll decide that when the time comes. We'll be arriving at . . . hmmmmm, it all depends on which route looks good.**

2. Hi, lab partner. Hey, the teacher says we're working on nitroglycerin today. What a blast! Should be easy enough. In fact, I didn't even bring my lab book. Hey, I figure I can just do my own thing.

3. I don't need instructions to nuke this TV dinner – just pop it in the micro-wave.

4. I don't need to follow the Bible to live a good life.

Transition

We're going to discover that God's instruction book is essential in finding out what's best for us.

2. Explore the Bible and Life

☐ Break into two or more groups. Have each group discuss one of the following Scripture portions:

Group 1: Romans 11:33–12:2

Group 2: 2 Timothy 3:16

Have each group discover the main point of the verses. Group 1 should find that God's instructions lead to His good, pleasing and perfect will. Group 2 should observe that all Scripture is valuable for spiritual growth and development.

Then ask the entire group these questions:

1. **Can we prove anything we want to using Scripture?**

2. **What are some ways people use God's Word to prove *their* point?**

3. **How can we "correctly handle" God's Word?** (Review the four points for effective Bible study.)

4. **React to this statement: God has given us the Bible, not so we can know *it*, but that we can know *Him*.**

5. **How does knowing God help us know right from wrong?**

3. Enact the Truth in Life

Ask teens to commit to reading one chapter of the Bible a day for at least the duration of this study.

Week 3: General principles
1. Is it beneficial?
2. Is it not mastering me?

1. Engage Interest

☐ Option 1
Bring in that stack of magazines that's been collecting in your closet. Have teens cut out pictures of various "things" and place them in one of two piles: "Good" and "Bad". Ask groups or individuals, **Why did you label these "things" as "good" and these things as "bad"?** Make transition into Bible study by saying, **Let's see how God divides "things."**

☐ Option 2
Play charades. Have four teens act out these words: **Nuclear reactor, alcohol, television, cyanide.** Make transition into Bible study by saying, **In acting out these "things" some showed the "good" or "bad" uses of them. Let's see how God looks at "things."**

2. Explore the Bible and Life

☐ Break into four groups. Have each group discuss one of the following Scripture portions:
Group 1: Matthew 15:10, 17-18
Group 2: 1 Corinthians 6:13-20
Group 3: 1 Corinthians 10:23
Group 4: 1 Timothy 4:1-5
Have each group discover the main point of the verses. Then ask the entire group these questions:

1. What do you think Paul means by "everything"?
2. Is everything permissible for the Christian?
3. Are medical discoveries moral or immoral?
4. Are scientific discoveries moral or immoral?
5. What makes something moral or immoral?

3. Enact the Truth in Life

☐ Have teens write out the benefits of their issue. Then write down possible destructive elements.

Week 4: General principles
3. Is it motivated by love?

1. Engage Interest
☐ Option 1

Read the opening monologue of the chapter as a five-year-old, or have one of your teens perform it.

☐ Option 2

Throw a Nerf ball to one of the students. When he/she receives it, have him/her complete this sentence: Love is . . . Answers needn't be completely serious: . . . a warm puppy. . . . changing a tire for a friend – in the rain – in your good clothes. He then tosses the ball to someone else who fills in the blank.

Transition

Today, we'll take a look at Paul's third principle for deciding if something is right or wrong for you.

2. Explore the Bible and Life

☐ Break into three groups. Have each group discuss one of the following Scripture portions:

Group 1: Matthew 5:38-48
Group 2: Matthew 22:34-40
Group 3: John 15:9-17
Group 4: Romans 12:9-21
Group 5: Romans 13:8-10
Group 6: Romans 14:19-23
Group 7: 1 John 3:16-19
Group 8: Revelation 2:1-6

Have each group discover the main point of the verses. Then ask the entire group these questions:

1. What are the four kinds of love mentioned in the book?

2. What kind of love are these verses talking about?

3. Why does *agape* love fulfill all the law?

3. Enact the Truth in Life
☐ Have teens privately write what motivates them to "wear purple sweat socks". Then have them ask themselves, **Are these pure motives? Are they loving (*agape*) motives?**

Perfect Love by Keith Drury, David Holdren, Jimmy Johnson, David Keith, Blair Ritchey, Richard Wynn and myself would be a "perfect" book to complement this and the next session. It too has a similar style and leader's guide for thirteen sessions. Available from Wesley Press for just $2.95.

Week 5: General principles
3. Is it motivated by love?
Part 2

1. Engage Interest

☐ Option 1
Play Amy Grant's "Love of Another Kind" from

her *unguarded* (Myrrh) album. Discuss, **What kind of love is she singing about? How does this differ from the "top-forty" kind of love?**

☐ Option 2
Bring a VCR recording of the top three songs or a list of the top forty songs for the current week to the meeting. Have teens share what kind of relationships each is presenting.

2. Explore the Bible and Life

☐ Draw a line dividing the board or overhead into two columns. In one column write the characteristics of the love found in 1 Corinthians 13. In the second column the characteristics of M-TV's kind of love.
Say, **This kind of love isn't based on warm, fuzzy emotions.** Break into four groups. Have each group discuss one of the following Scripture portions:
Group 1: 1 Corinthians 1:20-27
Group 2: Ephesians 4:14-15
Group 3: Colossians 2:2-4
Group 4: 2 Peter 1:5-9
Then ask the entire group, **What do these verses say about love and decision-making?**

3. **Enact the Truth in Life**

☐ Have groups or individuals write their own definition of love. Then have individuals privately answer question three on the chart in the back of the book.

Week 6: General principles
4. . . . clear conscience?
5. . . . not causing a weak Christian to sin?

1. Engage Interest

☐ Option 1
Begin by relating the story of "Rodent" from the chapter. Ask, **How would you react to this girl?**

☐ Kidnap her, wash and set her hair, shave her legs and haul her off to a Mary Kay cosmetics party?

☐ "See the light" and wear black dresses yourself and only wash your hair on Christmas and Easter?

☐ Other?

☐ Option 2
Bring in a pair of sweat socks. Say, **My mother's criterion for whether socks belonged in your drawer or the laundry basket was this: "If it's doubtful, it's dirty."**

Does that sound like a good principle for purple sweat socks? Let's take a look.

2. Explore the Bible and Life

☐ Read Romans 14:13-15 and 20-23. **What principles for purple sweat socks is Paul giving to us?** Then draw the chart from the chapter on the board and discuss each point.

Then read and discuss 1 Corinthians 8:7-13 and Matthew 18:6-8. Since this is a sensitive issue, it may be best to use the main points of this section as a mini-lecture.

3. Enact the Truth in Life

☐ Have teens individually work through a "hang-up"

using the chart. Stress that even if they know this is an irrational hang-up with no biblical basis, they should not do anything that produces tension, mental stress or a cloudy conscience.

Also point out the importance of considering "weaker" Christians in their wearing of purple sweat socks.

Conclude by having them individually answer questions four and five on their own charts.

Week 7: General principles
6. . . . a glory to God?
7. . . . good for my witness?

1. Engage Interest

☐ Option 1

Break into three groups. Have each group discuss items or activities that could be used to "bring glory to God."

☐ Option 2

Rent the video of *Chariots of Fire*. Show the clip where Eric is explaining to his sister how he feels God's pleasure when he runs. Eric believes he can glorify God by running.

2. Explore the Bible and Life

☐ Option 1

Break into two groups. Have each group discuss one of the following Scripture portions:

Group 1: Matthew 25:14-30

Group 2: Romans 14:16-18

Have each group discover the main point of the verses. Then ask the entire group these questions:

1. What do we mean by "bringing glory to God"?

2. What are some practical ways we can bring glory to God?

3. How do you react to the comment, "It's not the quality that counts but the spirit"?

4. How can we judge excellence?

5. What are some practical ways we can draw attention to God?

6. What are some things that non-Christians consider unchristian?

7. Make a list of activities you were involved in this week. Assign a 10 to "glorifiers," a 5 for "neutral," 0 for "detractors" and any in between. Are there some areas that could be improved?

☐ Option 2

Use the entire session time to view *Chariots of Fire*. The story of missionary Eric Liddle makes the two points of this session in a powerful way.

3. Enact the Truth in Life

☐ Have teens each write on a 3x5 card one thing they could do that would glorify God and draw non-Christians to Him. Encourage teens to mount it on their mirror at home as a reminder for the week.

Week 8: Does God change His mind?

1. Engage Interest

☐ Option 1

Make two signs. One should read **APPLAUD** and the other **BOO**. Ask one of your theatrical teens to read the following script. Introduce him or her by saying:

Ladies and gentlemen, as (teen's name)'s campaign manager, it is my privilege to introduce

the best candidate for the senior class – (teen)! (Hold up APPLAUD sign beside teen.)

(Teen): **Thank you, thank you, thank you. I'm running for president of the senior class. If I am elected, I propose to create better students by petitioning to have the school day extended by one hour.** (Hold up the BOO sign beside teen.)

However, on the other hand, my presidency may be able to accomplish the same goals by decreasing the school day by one hour. (Hold up APPLAUD sign beside teen.)

And I promise you, if elected, to clean up crime in our hallways. Anyone caught littering will be required to mop and wax the entire hall. (Hold up the BOO sign beside teen.)

But, on the other hand, these same objectives could be implemented by hiring extra janitors. (Hold up APPLAUD sign beside teen.)

On the international scene, if I am elected, I will work to free up monies for underprivileged schools. One way to do this is to eliminate dessert from the school lunch program. (Hold up the BOO sign beside teen.)

But, by campaigning hard to reprioritize the school's budget, it may be possible to provide T-bone steaks every Friday. (Hold up APPLAUD sign beside teen.)

And so in conclusion, if I am elected president of the senior class, I will not be dictated to by lobbyists, I will take my stand and not let public opinion influence my decisions. (Hold up the BOO sign beside teen.)

Yes, as I said, I will take your suggestions to the office with me, for I am *your* **candidate for senior class president, but most of all your friend. Thank you.** (Hold up APPLAUD sign beside teen.

Transition

(Name) certainly changed his/her mind. When

we read the Old and New Testaments, we might think God changes His mind quite often. Let's talk about that.

☐ Option 2

Place three signs in the meeting room. The sign on one end of the room should read **STILL APPLIES,** on the opposite end **DOESN'T APPLY,** and in the middle of the room **NOT SURE.** Ask teens to move under the sign that reflects their belief about the relevancy of the following Old Testament laws:

A believer should offer burnt sacrifices at the temple.

God hates divorce.

A follower of God shouldn't get a tattoo.

You shouldn't murder anyone.

If you break out in a rash, you should have your minister look at it.

A believer can't eat pork, but can eat grasshoppers.

A follower of God should never misuse His name.

Working on the Sabbath deserves the death penalty.

You should honor your mom and dad.

Anyone who curses his father or mother should be put to death.

A believer shouldn't charge interest when lending money.

A follower of God shouldn't lie.

A believer should never eat the fat around the edges of a steak.

Transition

How do we know what laws apply today, and what rules were just for the Jewish nation 4,000 years ago? Let's try to find out.

2. **Explore the Bible and Life**

☐ Break into three groups. Have each group compare

and contrast the following Scripture portions:

Group 1: Matthew 5:17-18/Romans 8:1-4

Group 2: Hebrews 7:23-27/Colossians 2:13-17

Group 3: 1 Timothy 1:8-11/Romans 7:7

Have each group discover the main point of the verses. Then ask the entire group these questions:

1. What are some things that were preached against as wrong in the past, which are now accepted as right?

2. Why is this so?

3. Does God change His mind on issues?

4. In what ways does the Bible *appear* to contradict itself?

5. How much of the Old Testament are we required to obey?

6. If we really love God and others as ourselves, do we need laws to make us do right?

3. Enact the Truth in Life

☐ Have teens individually write down an apparent contradiction. For "homework" ask them to explore the Scripture for passages that shed light on the situation.

Week 9: How can I hear God's Spirit?

1. Engage Interest

☐ Option 1

Have two or three volunteers (victims) go outside the room. While they are gone, rearrange the chairs into a maze. Divide the remaining group in fourths. When one of the volunteers returns blindfolded, one-fourth of the group is to call out correct instructions for navigating the chairs. The rest of the group is to yell out wrong advice. After the two or three victims have run the maze (more likely run into the maze), ask for their reactions.

Was it confusing having several voices calling out directions? Did you figure out which voices were telling the truth?

Explain that this is how it feels sometimes when we're trying to "find God's will" for our lives.

☐ Option 2

Brainstorm ways for "finding" or listening to God's will.

2. Explore the Bible and Life

Have half the group read Romans 12:1-2, and the other half read Proverbs 3:5-6. Have these buzz groups discover the principles for "finding" God's will.

Is God's will "lost" and something we have to "find"?

Ask, **How can we really "hear" God?**

3. Enact the Truth in Life

Have teens privately try the Inter-Varsity method for sorting out their thoughts. They should choose any decision that is facing them this week (or year). Allow plenty of time. It may work best if the group can find a quiet spot in the church to work on it. (If you do, *watch out* for teens who like to take advantage of unsupervised time.)

Close in a time of commitment or prayer for guidance.

This session development was reprinted by permission from *Perfect Love* © 1987 by Wesley Press.

Week 10: How can I be sure it's God's Spirit?

1. Engage Interest

☐ Option 1

Read the true situations at the beginning of this chapter. Ask, Have you ever heard similar cases of "God told me"?

☐ Option 2

Read the following letters I've received as an editor.

Dear Editor,

God told me to write this poem, but your publishing house rejected it. You rejected God's poem just before the tornadoes wiped out half your building in 1965. God is giving you a second chance to repent and publish my poem. God is giving you six weeks.

(Marion, Indiana)

Dear Editor,

God wrote this article. I don't even know what's in it.

(Fort Wayne, Indiana)

Dear Editor,

God told me to write this article. At least I think it was God. Maybe it was God. Maybe it was the devil. I don't know. Maybe you can tell me.

(Chino, California)

Transition

A lot of people are claiming to have a message from God. But how can we be sure what's from God and what isn't? Let's find out.

2. Explore the Bible and Life

☐ Review chapter nine by asking, **How do we hear**

God's thoughts? Then break into groups. Have each group (or each individual) explore one of the following Scripture portions:

    Group 1: Psalm 119:97-99
    Group 2: Proverbs 1:1-7; 2:1-2
    Group 3: Proverbs 3:5-6
    Group 4: John 14:25-27; 16:8-15
    Group 5: Romans 8:5-8
    Group 6: Romans 11:33–12:2
    Group 7: 1 Corinthians 2:6-16

Have each group discover the main point of the verses. Then ask the entire group these questions:

1. Do you think the people at the beginning of chapter ten really heard from God?

2. Where do you think they went wrong?

3. What four forces influence our thinking?

4. How can we "test" the spirits? (Use Martin Wells Knapp's checklist.)

3. Enact the Truth in Life

☐ Have teens write in their individual charts what they sense *God's* Spirit is telling them about purple sweat socks.

Week 11: The youth group and the church board

1. Engage Interest

☐ Option 1

Assign five teens to a different verse from Romans 14:19-23. Begin the session by saying, **I've asked five teens to each read one verse from Romans 14.** (You have previously cued them to each read their different verses at the same time.) The sound should be chaotic.

Say, **Ah, you all did well, but let's try all reading together in unison.**

☐ Option 2

Read the following real news article.

BURKE, Texas — **A** dispute over money that began three years ago among members of a fundamentalist church in Burke, Texas, continues today in a full-blown lawsuit.

The two factions of the congregation are fighting in court for the control of the Burke Pentecostal Church near Lufkin.

They're also fighting outside of court, with pranks such as squirting glue in church door locks, pouring olive oil in the organ, and more. And the community is fed up.

"If I thought I had the authority, I would order this church sold and have it closed down," state district judge David Walker said recently in court.

The Angelina County Sheriff says he has washed his hands of the congregation.

"In the last three years we've been called out there 70 or 80 times," Sheriff Sammy Leach Jr. said recently. "I finally told them there was nothing I can do. We will not answer a call out there unless somebody's bleeding."

The church membership has dwindled from 140, three years ago, to less than two dozen.

What is your reaction to the story?

What kind of influence do you think this church is having on the community?

How do you think God views this church?

Transition

Unity is important in the church. But does that mean that everybody has to agree on the issue of purple sweat socks?

2. **Explore the Bible and Life**

Ask the following questions:

1. **What causes disunity in the church? in teen groups?** (You may want to use this book's five points for a mini-lecture.)

2. Do purple sweat socks themselves cause divisions? Or is it people's reactions to purple sweat socks?

Break into small groups or into twos. Have each group explore the following Scripture portions:

Group 1: Matthew 7:1-5, 15-20
Group 2: John 17:20-23
Group 3: Acts 2:42-47
Group 4: Romans 2:1-4
Group 5: Romans 14:1–15:7
Group 6: 1 Corinthians 12:12-31
Group 7: Ephesians 4:1-6
Group 8: 2 Timothy 2:25-26
Group 9: James 4:11-12

Have each group discover the main point of the verses. Then ask the entire group, **How would following these verses create unity out of division?**

You may want to wrap up the session with the positive points for creating unity.

3. Enact the Truth in Life

☐ Have teens create banners or posters for the following thought:

In essentials, unity
In non-essentials, liberty
In all things, charity

Week 12: Friends and parents

1. Engage Interest

☐ Option 1

Have teens privately write what they feel is the hardest part about living, going to school, or working with non-Christians. Collect the cards and read them to the group. DON'T divulge who wrote each.

☐ Option 2
Come into the meeting room dressed in a white sheet proclaiming the joy of Kosgro McOrlo. (Make up a few points of McOrlo theology.)

Transition
It's tough trying to live out your faith and convictions with people who aren't sympathetic to them.

2. Explore the Bible and Life

☐ Option 1
Ask, **"Why don't Christians and non-Christians seem to get along well together?"** Break into two groups. Have each group explore one of the following Scripture portions:
   Group 1: Luke 12:49-53
   Group 2: 2 Corinthians 6:14-15
Have each group discover the main point of the verses. Then ask the entire group these questions:
Are there some things we could do to avoid unnecessary friction?
Have groups huddle again to explore these verses:
   Group 1: Colossians 4:5-6
   Group 2: 1 Peter 3:15-16
Receive their "report", then ask:
What ways can we "answer everyone" and "give the reason for the hope that we have"? (Use the three points at the end of the chapter as a mini-lecture.)

☐ Option 2
Invite someone from Campus Crusade or Young Life to teach your teens some ways to share their faith.

3. Enact the Truth in Life

Have the two groups work to "translate" the following terms into language an unchurched friend could understand: **saved, sin, redemption, fellowship,** "feel His presence," conviction, (add some more if you wish). In order to share the hope, we need to communicate clearly!

Week 13: Student Council and the Supreme Court

1. Engage Interest

☐ Option 1
Bring to class articles that report on government oppression of Christianity in Soviet or Moslem countries. Share these with your class.

☐ Option 2
Have the first week's "Ted Toppel" share this final segment from "Night Light."

Toppel: Good evening, and welcome to "Night Light". I'm Ted Toppel. Several weeks ago, we reported on the national obsession of purple sweat socks. As you recall, closed factories have been retooled and are now producing the purple profit makers. And exports of the colorful footwarmers have effectively reduced the trade deficit and brought unemployment under one percent.

Today, the President signed into law the Woolsitter Amendment making the wearing of purple sweat socks mandatory. The President stressed that for further economic growth and national unity, the wearing of purple sweat socks is the patriotic duty of every American.

The state and local branches of the Executive endorse the Federal legislation which would mean a 30-day jail sentence or 1,000-dollar fine for first offenders. For reaction we go to the (name of your church) youth group.

Transition

What if the government ruled you will wear purple sweat socks, but you felt God didn't want you to wear them? The Scripture reports several instances of people who ran into the same situation.

2. Explore the Bible and Life

☐ The small groups explore biblical examples of men who ran into problems with the government. Then have each explore Romans 13:1-7.

Group 1: Judges 6:13-32; Romans 13:1-7
Group 2: Daniel 3 and 6; Romans 13:1-7
Group 3: Matthew 17:24-27; Romans 13:1-7
Group 4: Acts 4:1-22; Romans 13:1-7
Group 5: Acts 5:17-42; Romans 13:1-7
Group 6: Romans 11:33–12:2; 13:1-7

Have each group discover the main point of the verses. Then ask the entire group, "**What are some practical ways to put Rutherford's four points into practice?**"

3. Enact the Truth in Life

☐ Have teens refer back to the chart they have been working on this past quarter. Encourage them to use the other charts as new issues come their way. And remind them, **If you don't think for yourself, someone else will!**

Issue:

Specific scriptures that relate to this issue:

General scriptures that relate to this issue:
- ( ) It is beneficial and constructive.
- ( ) It is not mastering me
- ( ) It is motivated by God's love for others
- ( ) It produces a clear conscience
- ( ) It will not cause a weaker Christian to sin
- ( ) It is a glory to God
- ( ) It is good for my witness

Thoughts I sense God gave me concerning this issue:

Actions I need to take as a result of my position on this issue:

Issue:

Specific scriptures that relate to this issue:

General scriptures that relate to this issue:
- (   ) It is beneficial and constructive.
- (   ) It is not mastering me
- (   ) It is motivated by God's love for others
- (   ) It produces a clear conscience
- (   ) It will not cause a weaker Christian to sin
- (   ) It is a glory to God
- (   ) It is good for my witness

Thoughts I sense God gave me concerning this issue:

Actions I need to take as a result of my position on this issue:

Issue:

Specific scriptures that relate to this issue:

General scriptures that relate to this issue:
- ( ) It is beneficial and constructive.
- ( ) It is not mastering me
- ( ) It is motivated by God's love for others
- ( ) It produces a clear conscience
- ( ) It will not cause a weaker Christian to sin
- ( ) It is a glory to God
- ( ) It is good for my witness

Thoughts I sense God gave me concerning this issue:

Actions I need to take as a result of my position on this issue:

Issue:

Specific scriptures that relate to this issue:

General scriptures that relate to this issue:
- (   ) It is beneficial and constructive.
- (   ) It is not mastering me
- (   ) It is motivated by God's love for others
- (   ) It produces a clear conscience
- (   ) It will not cause a weaker Christian to sin
- (   ) It is a glory to God
- (   ) It is good for my witness

Thoughts I sense God gave me concerning this issue:

Actions I need to take as a result of my position on this issue:

Issue:

Specific scriptures that relate to this issue:

General scriptures that relate to this issue:
( ) It is beneficial and constructive.
( ) It is not mastering me
( ) It is motivated by God's love for others
( ) It produces a clear conscience
( ) It will not cause a weaker Christian to sin
( ) It is a glory to God
( ) It is good for my witness

Thoughts I sense God gave me concerning this issue:

Actions I need to take as a result of my position on this issue:

Issue:

Specific scriptures that relate to this issue:

General scriptures that relate to this issue:
- ( ) It is beneficial and constructive.
- ( ) It is not mastering me
- ( ) It is motivated by God's love for others
- ( ) It produces a clear conscience
- ( ) It will not cause a weaker Christian to sin
- ( ) It is a glory to God
- ( ) It is good for my witness

Thoughts I sense God gave me concerning this issue:

Actions I need to take as a result of my position on this issue:

Issue:

Specific scriptures that relate to this issue:

General scriptures that relate to this issue:
( ) It is beneficial and constructive.
( ) It is not mastering me
( ) It is motivated by God's love for others
( ) It produces a clear conscience
( ) It will not cause a weaker Christian to sin
( ) It is a glory to God
( ) It is good for my witness

Thoughts I sense God gave me concerning this issue:

Actions I need to take as a result of my position on this issue:

Issue:

Specific scriptures that relate to this issue:

General scriptures that relate to this issue:
- (   ) It is beneficial and constructive.
- (   ) It is not mastering me
- (   ) It is motivated by God's love for others
- (   ) It produces a clear conscience
- (   ) It will not cause a weaker Christian to sin
- (   ) It is a glory to God
- (   ) It is good for my witness

Thoughts I sense God gave me concerning this issue:

Actions I need to take as a result of my position on this issue:

Other excellent books written by Jim Watkins and published by Wesley Press

Keeping Pace

Youth conventions, camps and rallies are like races that begin at the finish line with lots of enthusiasm and excitement. But soon after, many find themselves sitting on the sidelines until the next youth event. Here's a book to help teens keep in good spiritual shape . . . long after the last convention, camp or rally.

Perfect Love

Jim has joined Keith Drury, David Holdren, Jimmy Johnson, David Keith, Blair Ritchey and Richard Wynn in writing this exciting book on relationships. *Perfect Love* is designed to communicate a practical message of holiness to teens of the eighties.

The Persuasive Person

Would you like to communicate more effectively in person and in print? The author uses scriptural principles and psychological studies to reveal how to motivate your youth board, how to speak more effectively, how to increase giving and much more. Keith Drury calls it "intensely practical and occasionally hilarious."

To order, call 1-800-62-SALES